Meditations from the Lazy Susan
The Poetry and Prose of Keith R. Deshaies

Actazia Publishing

Meditations from the Lazy Susan

The Poetry and Prose of Keith R. Deshaies

Meditations from the Lazy Susan

Published by Actazia Publishing
515 116th Ave NE #249
Bellevue, WA 98004

Publisher Cataloging-in-Publication Data

Deshaies, Keith.
    Mediations from the lazy susan : The poetry and prose of
    Keith R. Deshaies / [edited by] Jennifer Deshaies.
    p. cm.
    ISBN 978-1-60756-001-2

1. American Poetry. I. Deshaies, Keith, 1964-2008 II. Title

PS301.326 2008
811

Library of Congress Control Number: 2008937611

Manufactured in the United States of America
Printing number: 10 9 8 7 6 5 4 3 2 1

Table of Contents

Foreword

When Keith died suddenly in 2008 at the age of 43, I, as his wife, had the daunting task of shuffling through years of journals, short stories, poems, and novels. To those of us who loved him, these are his words, his message, to us, to the world. He was such an talented writer, to hold these writings to myself seemed selfish. Keith's dream was to have his work published. He'd had work published several times, but not his personal work. Not the work that burst forth from his amazing intellect and unique view of the world around him. I often imagined the day we would get a box of his first novel in the mail, open a bottle of good red wine and celebrate. To me, this was inevitable. And so, as a tribute to him, I set forth to try to find the work that best encompassed Keith as a writer to share. The book you are holding is the result of that work. It is simply, a labor of love for the most extraordinary man I ever met.

He had turned toward poetry writing the last few years of his life with zeal. It is because of this and because it is the last of his work, that the majority of this book consists of poetry. You will find excerpts of his handwritten work throughout this book. As a teacher I found two things about his writing to be fascinating. His handwriting was impeccable and he rarely wrote more the one draft. He could craft a poem in his head in minutes and it would splash onto the page without so much as a misplaced comma. He did this as easily as breathing.

You will note that there are several poems that are untitled. Keith rarely titled a poem unless it was being published in some sense. Knowing him as well as I did, I still do not pretend to know what titles he would have chosen for his work. I say to you humbly that I am not, nor ever will be, the caliber of writer you will read in this book and therefore did not feel qualified or justified in adding even so much as a title to his work.

You might be wondering about the title of the book. Keith had written it as a header to some of the work I found. We would often use the term "the lazy susan" as a metaphor for Keith's brain because it had so much in it, and yet it would spin and spin until is splattered a mess everywhere.

My wish is for those of you who read this book to see something a little different in the world. Like Keith's writing, to find the voice to fight injustice, to revel in beauty of the mundane, the peace of self-reflection and the power of love.

And now, I am going to go open a good bottle of red wine, raise a glass to Keith and celebrate his success.

Acknowledgments from the Editor

Thanks to:

Kay, Pav, and Actazia Publishing for their generosity, guidance and care in creating this work. I would like to thank Kay Unkroth in particular for mentoring Keith with his writing, always pushing him, always believing in him. It meant much to him.

Rhonna, wherever she is, for helping Keith see himself as a writer.

Keith's family: To Jan, Ed, Keri, and Jonathan Jaworski and Marc, Janet, Adam and Leah Tanguay for embracing me as part of their wonderful family. To Claire, for giving birth to him. To his father Ray for giving Keith his humor. To Jan and Marc for loving and protecting Keith and helping him become such an incredible person.

Allan Krygeris for being such a true and wonderful friend to Keith for 20+ "odd" years and for the love and quiet support he has bestowed on me in Keith's absence.

My parents and my family. For everything. Your guidance and encouragement allowed me to become whole.

Tom and Anna Warnke. You are the blessings in my life. I would never had made it this far without your many years of love, support and friendship. I am forever grateful for the times of laughter, friendship, fun, and "oh dude!" the fearsome foursome shared together.

Misty Nikula for her expert editing skills, unconditional love and numerous phone calls that have gotten me through these last few months.

My friends and students who have seen me through tough times and keep me smiling.

Dedication

This book is dedicated to our children: Becca and Aaron Deshaies and Jake and Tessa Jones. It is a hard thing to lose your father when you, yourself, have really yet begun to live. I know from here on there will be many milestones without him: graduations, weddings, births. Know that he loves you, always. I hope, in some small way, this book helps you feel closer to him.

If we are to
save the world,
we must destroy
The Walls.

-Keith Deshaies
February, 2003

Poetry

The simple act of a pen
leaking dark blue ink
onto a cotton white page,
The simple act of a hand
dragging words all over the place
like a Radio Flyer red wagon
The simple act of a mind
concocting sentences from thoughts
following rules and margins
The simple act of a heart
reaching across miles
reaching across continents
The simple act of a soul,
breathing free in clean solitude,
following freedom down a green path
The simple act of concentration
of paying attention to the words
of the receiver's gentle hands
The simple act of talking quietly
spread over time over distance
morning sun over a wet valley
The simple act of giving time
giving consideration, sharing
an afternoon across ten time zones
The simple act of looking
of looking and finding we both breathe—
Together we share this earth.
This simple act of writing
with this pen this ink
with this time this love
So easy in a gesture, in a blink.

4/3/04   Home (Kent)

2

All They Have

Days-old stubble
roughs up his hands
as he chugs
the conspicuously wrapped can
of malt beverage.
Almost noon, but bleary-eyed
and reeking, he poses
no threat to folks
who walk by and stare,
clutching their lattes
and leather bags.
Somebody lived in that shell once.
Somebody loved that shell once.
The conversation between
he and his buddy blossoms.
They curse and slur,
spit pinwheeling everywhere.
Some grumbling some silence.
Unintelligible, they hug,
Dying a slow incoherent death,
as the little city thrives around them.
They try to stand.
A gentle spring breeze grabs
their shabby denim garb
and flings the scent of old urine
into the cool spring day.
They walk nowhere.

*First Place Winner for Poetry at the Write on the Beach 2003 conference

Hey, Baby

Sitting on one of those
twelve-thousand dollar crotchrockets,
he motions to the Sweet Young Thang
in the little blue Honda Civic.
"Sit here," he beckons,
tapping the pad behind him.
"Feel my power."
She flips her blonde locks
and shrugs a "Sorry" at him.
The light changes to green.

He's a 21st century James Dean:
A half-assed rebel
with causes to ignore.
"How could you not want THIS?"
He exudes, incredulous at her choice.
He wrenches the throttle,
leaving everyone behind,
spewing an image of purple,
white leather and Lycra
of exhaust and image,
all innocent pollution.
The young blonde drives on,
head bobbing to inaudible music.
She forgets, oblivious
I witness and report,
scratching my head,
grounded and grateful.

* Second Place Winner for Poetry at the Write on the Beach 2003 conference

Latte Girls

Their chatter perforates the ambient
Sounds of the bistro: In their twenties,
They spin the language of the day
And the language of relationships:
"Oh, it was totally unfair.
I just wanted to, like, hit him!"
I gnaw the remains of a stale cookie
While a mediocre latte lances my tongue,
And the two young women,
Clipped and coiffed, looking the part,
Unabashedly fling their inflections
And dubious postures, unaware
Of their voices forming the cheap
But brightly colored fabric
Of this moneyed microculture
I marvel at them as the coffee creation
Offers fine texture and savage flavor,
Their animated dialogue reaching
A flamboyant indignance:
"Yeah, but he called, right?"
"Not even."
"No way."
"Way."
I gag down the last of the bitter beige slurry
And observe their calculated prettiness,
Lurching between dirty old man
And wizened monk, the seductive smells
And curious sights flow with me
Through the big glass door, and they stride
Far ahead of me, continuing the banter
As it weaves itself
Into the day, the city, the world.

Downtown America

We see them all the time, you and I.
They touch us and evade us carefully.
Invite them in, and leave.

The bargain pundit, haranguing the barista
with the primetime newsbites,
animated beyond reason.

The Joe ordering Joe
at the other end of the counter,
barely opening his eyes or wallet.

The Russians in kerchiefs, piling in from the cold,
gathering at the menu board
happy to be here.

The well designed sage near the door,
Looking quite intelligent in ponytail regalia,
struggling with the Times crossword.

The cackler in the corner
responding to god knows what,
from his gnome-like friend.

The Oblivious sits by the window
staring at the traffic and gray street,
A mystery on the inside.

The goodtime old friend breezing in
smiling his way to the counter,
absorbing an embrace from the help.

The razor-thin woman in taut jans and leather accessories,
indulging in subdued pissed-off conversation
Encouraging discouraging attention.

A smug writer taking notes from Mars
Hoping that all of this stage
spawns a profound play.

Reprise

What if the fog clears?
What if, suddenly,
She stands there, smiling,
Ready to accept me
Without alteration, like pants
That need a little hemming here,
A little cuff there?
What if, after passion's rush ebbs,
We still sit together on the same couch
And still know each other
Without the need to hem and cuff,
Without the need to analyze and predict
The warm, cold, and occluded fronts
Of our weather map?
What if I look at the craggy old lady
And she looks at the craggy old man
And we can both smile the words
We thought of fifty years ago
When briefly, between storms,
The fog cleared?

Autumn

Autumn stole home this year.
Took my van, too.
Took all the leaves, and lots
of houses up North.
Red Sox missed by an inning again,
and the day of the floods
broke records for its rain and warmth.

Birthdays snuck up,
chased by Thanksgiving and Christmas.
We even wedged an anniversary in there.

And again I whine about my financial state,
my lack of writerly presence,
neoconservatives, reality TV,
and the Grand Wizard of Idiots
in the White House.
I fret about how little I enjoy,
bout the time I lack,
about everything out of reach
beyond my sphere of influence.

Sitting here in my truck
I open the window
to allow November's handshake.
I understand the balance and Now.
I see the evergreens and smell the **autumn**.
I understand, briefly, Now.

Our Classless Society

"Sir" causes a cringe.
I sit and write
Ten stories above
A calm warm harbor,
Watching gulls fight
On the stern deck rail.
"Sir" pushes me someplace foreign.
I know my roots:
Top Ramen, M&C,
And Gatorade for weeks on end.
Crappy car, when I owned one.
Studio apartment. Scraping by.
"Sir" pulls me back to now:
Deck Ten, Stern, sipping coffee
Delivered effortlessly
By a short Jamaican woman in pressed whites.
Honest pleases and thank yous
Bounce her way, but I wonder...
"Sir" suites me badly.
No knight, no king, no status,
Just a life's path I follow
And it happens to pause here now.
What I earn, who I earn:
Nothing more or less special
Than these gulls fighting on the railing in front of me
"Sir" reminds me of someone
Someplace sometime, some mind else.

Marathon

What fuels her incessant chatter
babbling flaccid minutiae
wondering aloud of traffic,
fretting pointlessly over weather
or the shallow utterly confident
expertise of a distant observer?
Neither pretty nor hideous,
the profoundly nondescript
foreground personality inserts
a disposable clarity in the moment:
"Wow. This traffic sucks
for such a sunny day."
A real intellectual reach, that.
More than this, though: It persists.
Marathoners and yoga masters: Take note.
Entire stories with no inward breath,
Downward Dog, or second wind.

Soon it transcends annoyance.
Soon it becomes epic.
The sun bakes the car's interior-
Window open, still no air.
She simply builds momentum,
not a second wasted.
She swings from sentence to sentence,
topic to topic, like a macaque
in tepid jungle. My presence
merely fortuitous, she soldiers
on about traffic, time, weather and crowds.
I finally say goodbye.
I drop her off, wondering
if she yet recites the litany of the obvious.
For her kind, though, I wish
them peace, and the possibility
of a talking meditation.

Today's Man

All right:
Beautiful woman on your left,
Earbud in you canal
Vacant look on your empty face
Empty buzzwords expectorated
effortlessly, as if they matter.

If a brain occupies her head,
may she bolt from Starbucks
with her grande chai before
it cools down, before
she succumbs
to the vacuous world of drivel,
of gain over substance
away from the distinguished
airhead with the thousand dollar
wardrobe, the five hundred dollar
wireless wonder in your ear,
and the classy personage you stole
from talk radio and Glitz TV.

May she leave you dangling
with that thing dangling from your ear
or that thing dangling
from your pants
as if your disposable persona mattered,
as if your thoughts suddenly waxed pithy
as if the relaxed fit chinos hid
the disposable manhood
or the cashmere hid
the girlish breasts
or the trendy jargon hid
your vapid store of knowledge.

May she run and try again,
find a live smile,
a barely disguised lust,
a genuine curiosity,
a giggle, a guffaw,
unabashed abandon in the real moment.
Leave the self-absorbed gadget genius
and write her life with pen, ink
build it with heart, stone, wood, love.

My Little Girl

Small and skinny,
long legs and big heart,
the Somewhat Present Sweetheart
lopes down the carpet runway,
bounces and flails
off the springboard,
gingerbread gymnast in space.
She waves and shouts to me,
unaware, unconscious of others,
of image, of anything except
nine year old joy,
gangly pure love
and boundless energy.
Just my girl and me.

New Year, Same World

Brave new year
New world
Old world
Same jammed planet
With six billion
Of the same stories
And dogma
Plodding and spinning
Celebrating our dominance
Of time and space
Of weather of rivers
Of oceans of nothing
Building our grand castles
And skyscrapers and malls
And institutions of nothing
Its predictable impermanence
Glittering and glowing,
Drops
Like the big Times Square Ball.
I smell tomorrow behind
The commuter-filled bus -
Offensive, then gone.

Vacation

Before the day awakes,
before the tension cranks up
like an old klaxxon,
herding us all to our
commuter mugs and bus passes;
before the streets teem
with the parasitic ooze of commerce,
and mangled tension
of efficient relaxation
in the forced power workout at noon;
before subordinate reports to superior;
before the Day of No Touching begins:
Remember the trapped warmth
of your blankets, your bed, your lover;
savor the tousled maniac in the mirror;
revel in the sleep-slurred goodbye
and slip quietly away
into morning dark, carrying
what really matters
On your lips, your gloves
in your coat pocket.
Protect it, protect you,
And stock vigilance
for the approaching day.

11/23/03
Whidbey Island, WA

Santa Claus

I rub my eyes,
I see snowflakes and dark
I see no colors
I walk I run I write
I try so hard to catch up
with you The kids Myself
I try to live professionally
I try to live simply
I try to just be
Cold and sweating,
I dart past
Finish line after finish line
Of red tape and artificial hoops
And closed doors.
I suck money
From the Great Corporate Teat
American DreamMare
They pay I pay we all pay
Too much too little
Attention we all need never get
Like the gallon of water a day
Like the vitamins we never take
Like the soil laid barren
Like the apologies left silent
Like the sudden understanding
Of all those kids who finally
Grasp the real identity
Of Santa Claus.

The Rhino

His toupee rustled gently,
Like a lazy squirrel,
munching acorns in October.

He holds the key to millions,
His ignorance of consequence
rivaled only by profound detachment.

Good for business, good for me,
He reports to the shareholders.
Good for business, good for you.

Expenses: Thirty species a day.
A rain forest here and there.
Some expendables in Sri Lanka.

He smugly announces triumph:
Sales up, despite the economy,
thanks to you, your sweat, my greed.

Somewhere Kenya, maybe,
On the shimmering veldt:
The Rhino slowly lifts his head.

The Rhino, threaded in life's web,
at the edge of the parched water hole,
Slowly lifts his head, knowing all.

Solstice #15

Gray flannel sky
Returns to your home,
This place you landed on
Fifteen years ago.
Yes, that long.
Among your accomplishments:
Unemployment, employment,
Marriage, two kids, vasectomy, divorce;
House in small town,
Apartment in city;
Writing and shutting up;
Shutting up and writing;
No addictions; must drink coffee;
No passions-
Well, not true.
Always the railroad,
Always the desire
To show and tell
Those who listen,
Those who care,
Those who feel rain's beauty
In a silver morning,
That you think of these things
And try to listen to each moment
And delight in good food,
Savor blue skies
And cherish new friends
As you share you new home, old home.

Old Friends, New Friends

Dark places on the water
Puget Sound deep and cold.
Blackness interrupted night
crashing passively on ragged shore.
Winter settles in, cold blanket
wrapping four friends
in a small island house;
threat of snow welcome
against a futile backdrop
of Workingworld, Mondayworld,
bleak promises of capital happiness
all dwarfed by the immense
warmth of the little house
on the little bluff
above the benign waves,
evergreen dark black shadow
odd foreboding flagging attempts
to shirk the other worlds we know,
we know too well.
Time to reflect, hold each other,
play dumb games, drink too much,
eat too much, share too much,
never enough, there exists never
enough. We must live here always.
Always now, always present.
Cooking together in little bright
kitchens with savory smells
and rich fragrant thyme.

Northwest Yule Muse:
A Transplant's Tale

Stays green here most years;
Christmas seldom turns white.
We only share commercialism
with the remaining forty nine,
and maybe the lingering
Judeo-Christian tradition or two.
The fruitcake. The mistletoe, The guilt.
The toddies. The hot buttered rum.
The uncomfortable silence, sitting
among relative seldom visited.
Sip something, wipe something.
Yes, we enjoy these things, too.

But the rain persists here, failing elsewhere.
No moss gathers there; here, roofs
blanket themselves in verdant velvet
while arsenals of zinc await
in home improvement stores,
where men grunt in strange tongues.
Buy in bulk, do it yourself, save big bucks.
Green on ground: Good. Green on roof: Bad.
Yes, we enjoy these things, too.

Years of acclimation, the persistent
lack of snow, Jack Frost nipping
at a latte in the mall, really laid-back,
and all the plaid Eddie Bauer encounters -
Years of absorbing this caffeine-drenched
woodland escapade garners no more
from me than a sigh, a shrug, a smile.

Storm

Scattered leaves, scattered time:
Old Glory straightens out those stripes
against a mottled gray sky,
stiff late fall wind forcing collars
up around cold red ears.
Downtown little town,
Northwest small town
Square corners, lazy streets
the hub the malls sabotage.
Traffic lights keep polite pace
baristas keep polite pace
barbers keep to meet greet repeat.

Scattered people, scattered time:
Elements of night in this day,
dark for noon downtown,
deep shadows in the maples,
just ahead of the holidays,
calm enough for November,
just before the Santa storm.
Still deciding in the promising gloom
whether to display a relaxed smile
or show the dispassioned stare
our evolutionary cynicism demands,
I sip my coffee as the autumn leaves
dance across the street under cars;
slip on my gloves and leave
the coffee shop bustle,
consulting the clouds, Old Glory,
the shadows, the maples, the people.

The Muse

The wire-haired bitch terrier
commenced pissing in my ear
rude incantations, affirmations
of talent of purpose of meaning
even before I woke up today.
She smells like an old crone's apron:
Hash brown leavings and bacon grease
dried in the pockets
smeared on the chest,
She understands nothing except: Drive.
I keep expecting, at least,
at the very least
a truck-stop-attractive waitress type,
full-breasted and road weary,
replete with "honeys" and "sugars"
and the clichéd wisdom of trucker life.
What passes for reality
shoved me elsewhere badly:
Reeking greasy stringy-haired crone
voice like a hinge
face like a coconut
body like a car crash
peg-legged walk.
I waddle about the house, disheveled,
I find a pen, a notebook
as the crone watches,
one glass eye, foul breath wafting,
she admonishes my lack of focus,
lack of drive
lack of discipline
lack of slenderness
lack of talent
lack of control
She throbs in my head.
She follows me into the day
to someplace warm and coffee infused;

the notebook, the pen plop on the table
Convinced, she disappears for now.
I sigh.
Normal people thus unafflicted
see this gesture as "settling in,"
"Relaxing with a cup of coffee."
No. No. No.
Glad the bitch left
for another few hours.

Tuesday

Grumbled to work one morning,
Whining about the job
And what fails inside.
Cool fall morning
And talk radio babble
Skewed toward the surreal:
I cannot believe it
I will not believe it
I dare not believe it
But I see it:
The 757 disappearing
Into Tower Two
Quietly, from here -
A fist in a pillow.
Over and overcoming
My denial shatters
With those lives, interrupted
By the manifestation
Of twisted Islam.
My pettiness shrinks
To the background
Of lives vanishing
So loudly, so publicly
Into the rubble of terror.

Migraine I

Jammed plumbing
Meets fractured light
The dull throbbing pain
Of avulsion, contusion
Of laceration, broken bone
No place to fit
No room for the intruder
Who hammers, mashes,
Pries, stabs, and lunges
Who insists on a table setting
At this banquet in Hell
He casually bludgeons
Other guests to death
He hates the light and heat
And whatever you eat
He tosses back on the table
Like a rude old fart
In a cheap strip mall deli
You long for the prescribed serenity,
The suede listlessness to take hold,
To escort this prick from the kitchen
You want to beat him to death
You want to crush this bastard's
Rotten heartless chest
But he glides away
Into his rancid darkness
To wait for another opening.
He waits.

Migraine II

Your eyes blink and squint
Harsh daylight, roomlight, whateverlight,
Burning the bedraggled brain awake
You hope the bastard left-
Just beat you senseless and left
You there, eyes half open,
Half comprehending.
Your deodorant too powerful, Your shirt too bright
Your news too loud
You pretended not to notice
But he drove the wedge,
He pounded relentlessly
Through your mind, your life.
Casually beating you
Into sleep, fearsome submission.
For three hellish hours
Bossing demanding, smashing
Your life to the three basics:
Cold, dark, quiet.
Nothing else mattered.
Nothing. No one.
You know he returns -
But please, not now.
Leave that head alone.
One day. Please.

A Means of Conveyance

They elude me:
Big blocks of polished metal
Plastic, fiberglass, shiny rubber
They feed the addiction
of our capitalist state.
We feed the beasts
We care for them
like stereotypical toy poodles.
We name them, use them,
Make them sleep outside
polish them change their fluids
assign them anthropomorphic value
show them off like big fluffy
Bichon Frises at Westminster.
We accessorize and glamorize
glorify and mollify,
we keep the Middle East
in control of us when we fill up.

When they break, I show
glimmering ineptitude:
I wring my hands.
Like some cosmic penalty
or fine of the incompetent,
I always pay three hundred dollars,
The Divine Invoice.
Others race them fix them build them.
To these mingling deities I pay my fine.
I maintain this strained relationship.
I pay the fines. The beast keeps me safe.
I speed to work. I see my kids.
I haul beauty bark. Pay the fines.

Occasionally, a flood
of testosterone breaches my pituitary
when idling at a stop sign.
I look to see if anyone notices.
Me. My truck. All the same.
The tide ebbs.
Embarrassed, I glide away.
I slink back into traffic
I think of what happens
under that massive hood
I take comfort in quarks,
string theory, and quantum mechanics.

Northwest Christmas

Once in awhile
As the winter digs in
And the dank rusts your joints;
As the days darken
When the whistle blows,
And your moods wade
In the kelp with the tides,
The spirit makes inroads,
Pierces the cold,
When that goofy kid smiles
When you hear the original carol
When "ice blue"
Really means "daylight on frost"
When money becomes paper and metal,
When lovers' gloved hands
Clasp and wing with their walk
And time and fir boughs
And bells and snow's quiet
All land together
Right now.

Ode to Middle Management

Droning incessantly,
You still manage to make no sense.
Your jargon irritates,
Like denim underwear.
You spew effortless meaninglessness
Like a baby effortlessly soils a diaper.
What sort of brain creates this?
What sort of mind?
Monotone and inane,
You captivate and inundate,
you babble and strain,
you slaughter innocent words
minding their own business,
while you build up yours.
An unclean chicken coop,
complete with spatter and smears,
Little downy feathers
and multicolored guano,
little predigested language pellets:
Your mind on buzzwords.

Oh, please, sire. More.
Grace me with your
Eloquence-free speech.
Your anesthetic banality.
Tell me again how to be
proactive, how to think outside
the goddamn box,
run this one up the
fucking flagpole so the big dogs
know who plays hardball.

Just show some mercy, for once:
show up on time, stop at two hours,
refrain from "going forward."

Rerun

Not again:
I saw CNN CBS NBC Fox ABC CNBC
And the 757 hit Tower Two over and over,
I saw the Daisycutter demo
I saw the carnage in Kandahar
I heard the accounts of the first attempt
twelve years ago,
And the nightvision view
of sheep or soldiers
scattering into the dunes of Iraq.
They insist, though:
His fault. Not ours.
Minimal casualties for our side.
Quiet and surgical
from thirty thousand feet,
Smart and accurate
from dozens of miles away
So clean from my living room.

Soon: Live images of death.
We kill from afar, on High Most High,
Self Appointed Christ Almighty.
Soon: Dresden or Nagasaki.
Stolen oxygen, scorched families
in Mosques, kitchen and backyards,
all hotly frozen forever,
our own industrial Pompeii.

I track one missile
To one building
Thanks to onboard
FighterVision Video
Not so clean
When other report
Not so quiet
When mothers scream,
Not so smart
When villages disintegrate
Not so stealthy
When bottomfeeders broadcast.
Just turn off those lives.

Not for oil
Not for God, Allah,
Our way of life,
Safety, Democracy -
No. Not again.

Radio News

I peaked today.
Saturated.
Accepting no further input.
Off. Shut. Out. Gone.
Talk to the eggplant.
Over wires, through air,
in waves, by discrete signal,
it permeates your being,
like Black Lung and the coal miner.

The sound of the day
The news of the dead
The oratory of plastic actors -

Three stories repeated
repeated every half hour,
painful sameness, different voices,
same sources, different prices,
disjointed, distended, disembodied;
death, toothpaste, war flatulence, maiming -
no matter for these empty-headed
conduits of informational effluence.
Just turn on the pump.

The halfhearted humor
and idiotic banter;
the Platonic NewsCouple
and their smarmy quips
infiltrate my car, my home, my space.
Auditory macaroni and cheese, AM. FM.
Channel 1,2,3,4,5, six billion.
I lost patience today. I found "Off."
I used it well.

The silence of the day,
The news of the Nothing.
The drive-by, self-inflicted quiet...

Year Ender

A year, a season dissolves
behind me, an inch for the kids,
bigger forehead for me.
Across the sea,
more suicide bombers,
more presidential bravado,
leaning on the podium
threatening the weak,
ignoring treaties, propping
up the wealthy.
We jam our SUVs
We carol, we cajole,
We travel, we feed like ravenous
cattle on the open range,
we sip nog and cider
as the year dips
below the horizon,
thick insulation of money
of time protecting our groggy
ignorance for another year.
Skip the year end eulogies like this one.
Skip the torment
of the ascetic family visits
and the lethal fruitcakes
and dinner experiments.
Concentrate.
Love now with all your
hands and lips and words.
Carry this past the setting sun.

The Reality of TV

It tells us what to think
what to buy what to feel
who to love who to hate
how to think how to trust
who to buy who to trust
when to exercise what to eat
who to exorcise how to eat
how to look what to love;
It shows us how to live
how to love, who to tell
who to show how to trust
when to lie what to lie,
when truth works who to kill
how to litigate when to mitigate
when to buy when to sell
what to drive who to sell
It entertains us enlivens us
enriches us and kills our kids
It addicts us, warms us,
soothes our conscience,
keeps us guilty, poverty-stricken, dead
It brings news, life, laughter.
It binds, divides, interacts,
detracts, sells, swells,
pays people billions of dollars
to play boy games, board games.
It sells toothpaste, drugs,
fun surgeries, lifestyles, too.
Lifestyles, lives so out of reach,
they exude comedy quickly countered
with carefully packaged reality.
Reality. It delivers reality.

12/22/03

The Kids Asleep

Silent house so rare,
So many, reaching back:
the tight-fisted family room.
On the unkempt Bellingham street,
the tension, the blasting
woodstove heat, the thick tensions,
the sparse apartments, the bar
wood, the cheap reek of particleboard,
particle life, temporary footbridge
to a better place, better time.
The four flights of stairs,
the flimsy smelly
postage stamp "balcony"
the third world old world charm
the twelve-square-foot fitness center
the hazmat-grade chlorine pool
and the stern hygiene warnings and rules.
The loud parking lot incarcerations
all neatly tucked into Suburbia
behind the HondaHyundaiFordHummer
dealerships with the inflatable gorillas.

And now:
the open family room with wood floors,
the last lights in the house
touching the snoring dog.
The last lights in the house
barely able to ward off sleep.
A world away from that old apartment world.
Sleeping kids now, snow scratching the windows,
the wind hushing the old tensions
away far beyond the old years, old fears.
The last light in the house
last sounds of the day,

the snoring dog, my loud head,
this pen on the hapless notebook.
A final meditations, meditation for peace.
Quiet now, Listen to the nothing.

All Aboard

The ferry's horn blasts me
Out of a wish, out of a daydream
As I sit in a glass shelter
By the tracks: Take me back,
Please, I enjoyed it:
Entangled hotly in abandon
By a rustic fire, crickets
And crackles, our breath a symphony,
Pine and fir, your hair, fallen leaves -
I breathe that life in and out,
Vague taste of red wine shared earlier
Clings softly to your tongue,
Hope, wonder, life and essence
Blaze from your eyes
As you see my future through a voice
Without words – Oh,
You sound so beautiful...
The appropriateness of the freight train
Shakes me literally to consciousness,
Rendering the ferry offshore a tame oboe,
Big, fast, heavy, unstoppable.
Red tail light blinks elusively
Into the distance, and like my dream
Disappears around a curve.

Moving Background

A five-year gulf
of time and freeways
decrees and expletives
disappears in the rear view
three hundred thousand miles
of I-5 and nomadic roots,
bleary-eyed visits with unknowing
cherubic kids a hundred miles
and three counties, to giggle with them
in a smelly Dairy Queen.
then mediate at 70
headed south for two more hours.

All of it falls away now,
the Skagit moon diving
into the velvet purple of dusk.

Fluke and fate guide me back
along the same interstate via
a very different route,
even Rand McNally overlooked.
Slightly older kids.
Slightly wiser me.
Still the trepidations.
Still the cold memories.
Still, I drive there,
Car, van, now truck
New life, new mind,
Old road, new road,
Same love. Same love.

Gathering of Angels

They cluster together
along the tracks
in outdated red down coats
baseball caps and sleeping bags
from not-quite REI
and a few letters short of LL Bean.
They find a bench to share stories.
They find a bench to make camp.
They find a bench of unity.

They disclose, one by one:
The Native American in red down,
day-to-day, and Express Personnel worker,
not quite sober.
The red-faced skinny one
in the denim jacket, still on disability,
but soon to make amends,
soon to really try at Step Four;
The pale white girl in simulated
leather jacket just smokes, just stares;
The curly-haired young one
counsels the rest on the S&P 500
As the spot in his pants
grows bigger and darker.

Crossing gates descend, bells ring.
A long loud train blasts through,
obscuring the troupe. Boxcars, hoppers,
container, flats. I watch their feet
between the cars, between the steel wheels.
I wonder at their families, lives, hopes, loves
what separates them from me.
A coincidental chill spreads
through my chest.
Not much, I think. Not much.
The last car flies through

the crossing, a blinking
red marker in its coupler.
Disappears.
I look for my story subjects.
Gone, too.
Such a fine line.
Such loud noises.
Such a long train
to disappear, meaning nothing.

Mazatlan

The pelicans swirl and circle
above the dry cliffs of Mazatlan
We only see the city they show.
We only find the fun we seek.
We tour bus by the shacks
and the dirt floor houses.
Corpulent American tourists,
we feed the squalor
by the boatload,
so self-unaware, unable
even to feel somewhat guilty.
We pour money into Mazatlan,
unaware of what it means,
who it serves, who it severs
as the pelicans and albatross
look for silver leaping fish
as Mazatlan hopes for
a new way, by the shipful.
Setting sun over Mazatlan,
street hawkers vacate
the tourist-swollen streets,
dissolve into alleys and hovels
waiting for the next
boatload of hope,
pelicans swirling, perching
on thick mooring lines
of hope.

Tourists

We push away from these warm cities,
our ancestors generations,
their ancestors
created long ago recently remember.
Bloated pasty white ankles caressed
by warm azure foamy silken sandy surf.
As cocoa brown relaxed smooth bodies
glide by on griddle white hot sand,
ambivalent about the others' presence.

My land your land
uneasy broken bilingualism
John Huston deserves praise
or punishment or accolades
or admonishment no time to think -
Eighty years of merciless construction:
some grateful, some not, I bet.

The ship pushing away from the dock,
bigger than most Puerto Vallarta skyscrapers,
contains self-contained ignorance
self-professed righteous absolution:
We cooperate, we employ,
we help those people, see? They smile!
We say hasta la vista, Puerto Vallarta.

We push away from the huge dock,
privilege looming over the rooftops,
propellers churning the muck of the bay,
returning to our own muddled opulence,
effervescent waters,
fading into warm dusk.

Airport, San Diego

Swirling homogeneous bustle
cram you through the scanners
lose the ring, the watch.
Scan that, too: All suspect.
Every last person and thing.
Yes, jam you through that check point.
Then: Wait. Oh, look! Over there!
Eight square feet of floor!
Drop my flabby white ass
on shabby gray carpet.
Prime real estate for three more hours.
Viewing traveler life at Bag Lady level,
wondering at all arrivals and departures,
scanning faces, attaching stories,
staving off headaches and hunger,
mindgames chasing boredom, frustration.
Stench of cologne convection
and of course, the Pizza Hut Express.
Steady din of travel jargon
in all languages, incessant, redundant.
All different, all the same.
Carry-on, walk-on, wheels behind
almost music, always loud.
No time for silent mind empty space:
National Guard soldier patrolling,
armed and ready nervous protection
No quiet no empty no mind:
Just the New Normal.

A Day in the Mind

Vacation, vocation
the calling the listening
the incompatibility
of expression and capitalism
this freedom we espouse
this wondrous money machine
distances self from soul,
render the difficult improbable.
I write, therefore I am.
Neat cliché with poor pay. I write, therefore I vanish.
I write anyway.
Stories, poems, journals, reviews
I keep flexing, stretching
racking my tiny stone garden,
mental tea ceremonies,
emotional insurance, resume'
of a life, nobody hiring, not soon.
I persist, whining, hand-wringing,
knowing nobody reads or cares anymore.
Leave it for archaeologists, then.
I play the odds with them:
Somebody understands.
Maybe not now, but then-
Sufficient recompense for true love,
ample reward for altruistic aim.
Don Quixote with a laptop.
And yet, I appreciate currency.

Loners

Well, now what?
You bask in your solitude,
surrounded by others.
Naked in public, in private.
You fear the freakishness
the craving implies -
A drug, a refuge, a habit?
Normal people behave better:
Parties, crowds, bars, malls.
They congregate on benches,
they chat in checkout lines,
they contemplate, holding hands
in churches, synagogues, temples.

You pray in the House of Latte,
guided by the Journal and
Notebook Most High,
Jesus Christ!
The difference, the "specialness"
remains appalling in the vast
overt nuclear forcefield
of "personal space" you lug around
like a cop's riot gear.

What drives you?
What drives you in your need?
The absolute necessity of roping off
the crime scene, dead zone, DMZ,
No Man's Land.
When to bridge the moat?
You decide, fair castle.

Critical Mass

Life's torn edges, worn out binders
pages filled with aimless words:
No, son, it ain't pretty.
When it makes sense, quit;
When chaos rules, dig in.
They teach me what I know
So I learn from myself;
questions mean more than answers.
Imagination over intelligence.
Value those who care,
overpay greedy idiots.
Seek good news; feast on bad.
We reside on a cake
frosted with knuckle-dragging lunatics.
Critical mass-
Yin and Yang saturation,
no room in the head,
for improvement, reproach, concern
or a brain-dead teen cashier's blank stare...
I drink Snapple absent-mindedly,
heedless of flavor or carcinogens,
unable to liberate my vast cranium
and its immense contents
from my own clenched buttocks.

Last Run

Time sprinkled his beard
with black and white,
coal flecks in the snow,
as he stepped
with awkward grace
exposing his well-earned limp
and thick-soled left boot,
he smiled privately
to the variegated crowd
that never noticed him, savoring
the ancient fragrances
of the big yellow engine
laboring loudly, even at idle.
He lumbered cautiously
over four rails and ballast,
the faint smile still creasing his eyes
as the old Alco rattled in the background.
He seemed to listen to it above
the noise of the crowd as he
slipped into the restored station
for coffee between tourist runs.
The station, the locomotive:
the only living beings older than he
in the whole scene.
He reappeared, paper cup in hand,
ambled back to the loud colleague,
grabbed a handrail, and murmured:
"Ten more miles, old girl.
Ten more miles."

Wages

She earned that smile,
the one she flashed
to the young unpretty
awaiting her latte.
The smile emerged easily,
the chemical blonde mane
stroking tan shoulders,
every step easy, flawless,
the creases near the mouth
showing joy, wages of a life
lived hard and strong,
deep green and red floral tattoo,
wrapped carefully around
her sinuous, sensuous ankle,
likely an ostentatious, careful dare,
brutal passion in unbeautiful places;
Men of the "supposed to's"
Boys of the "should haves"
Dark and furtive aggression,
road trips and outdoor concerts.
She orders, picks up, leaves,
lavender soft silk chemise
caressing the shoulders once more,
a "Thank you" and a warm smile,
calm independence,
nodding to the young unpretty
offering again the well-earned smile,
flowing into the afternoon sun.

Winter Passing

The sunny bleak sky
pierced the old barn
silently, relentlessly
as the unexpected cold
stilled all the inhabitants.
Snow swirled about the entrance
and a leathered weathered boot
crossed the threshold.

The heft of the five-gallon bucket
stiffened his right arm straight down
and he held the other straight out.
He balanced his way
through the setting sun in the barn,
the settling cold in the dearth,
the scattering cats in his path.
He found the old swayback
kneeling, asking politely for mercy
in his final hours minutes seconds.
The balancing stopped.
The bucket rested.
The glove dropped.
Wisps of heat rose from the knurled
knuckles, and concentration
more powerful than cold or sorrow
gathered in him as he thrust
the fist slowly into the sorghum-
sweetened oats, the last supper
of sorts for this trusted dying friend.

Understanding the scene, the setting,
the mottle gray horse edged toward
the smell, pitifully, selflessly
hoping to reach the human.
A taste. Maybe two.
The big rough tongue

warmed the big rough hand.
One last time.
No sadness for either elder.

The old steed settled
slowly onto his side,
still saying goodbye
with the dignity of a patriarch.
The mash, still dripping
from the big red mitt, hit
the concrete floor scattering bits
of straw and sawdust, soon the only
sound in the barn.
The massive ribcage shuddered
one final time in the thickening
shadow, and a life froze forever.

The red hand wiped itself
on stiff overalls, stuffed itself
in a hard leather glove.
The old man ambled
toward the snowbound door,
inhaled sharply, tucked his chin
to his chest, and pushed
into the snowy dusk, headed
toward the house,
footsteps disappearing behind him.

Focus Group Weather

The happy barking poodle
on Channel Five salivates
at the prospect:
A genuine snowstorm! Soon!
Reporters live on the scene!
Well, a reporter.
In front of traffic.
No snow in sight.

Be soon! Brace yourselves!
A hellish commute tomorrow!
Dead people on benches!
Frozen puppies! Lost grampas!
The city shuts down!
Her spackled, coiffed, talking head
nears orgasm with the momentum
of her Armageddon story:
More live reports!
Now, from our Doppler
RealFeel Extended five day
pinpoint Accucasting Weathermatic
Extravaganzoid Weather Center!
A real snow event!
The poodle slumps, spent.
Just in time for a commercial.

I look outside.
Cold. Dark.
Lazy flakes descend
in ones and twos.
Three inches max,
if it snows all night
and part of tomorrow.
Absorbing the magnitude
of the weathercast
and its neatly packaged
fear bundle, I scratch
my buttocks, shake my head,
and meander toward bed,
pausing to create Dark TV.

Distraction

We try to converse.
A radio phrase
a TV ad
an insipid song
We look away.
We try to return.
Probably need Prozac
Gingko biloba ginseng
Green tea yoga helps
Try Tai-Chi
I know a GREAT teacher
at the community college-

We blink a few times.
We try to return.
We try to converse anew.

Cars pass by.
The new hybrid
gets fifty mile a gallon.
I like my SUV.
Eco-Terrorist!
Bleeding heart greenie tree-hugger!
Apologies accepted.

We try starting over.
We try to converse.
We sip lattes.

We should try chai.
Much better for you.
Slated for Carcinogen City someday.
Everything causes cancer.
In one ear out the other.
A bunch of scare tactics.
I know somebody with cancer

Me too
How depressing
Oh, look: Zoloft samples!
Must we medicate everything?
My friend, the doctor -
Never trust 'em -

Some blank staring.
We try to return.
We sip. We breathe.
We notice gentle snow
outside the big cafe window.
We notice the absence of others.
We notice,
We smile.
We sip.

Persistence

Hope clings infernal,
scratching at the screen door,
dumb cat in the heat
of a desert night,
outlasting presidents
and governments,
earthquakes and divorces,
modern art and movie love.

It shows up in kids
dreaming of planets
and kids dreaming
of Earth, whole and clean,
and grownups who refuse
to consume a swath ahead
to leave a wake behind.

It arrives deep in the night,
a hand that heats the cool flank
under a blanket, melting
the cold words
of the argument before.

It slows the day's manic pace
and lifts your eyes
to yet another impossible sunset,
burning hot, infernal,
full of hope.

Day After Thanksgiving in Suburbia

The doors burst open
and a flood
of estrogen-laced capitalism
crashed through the narrow
portal into a festering
wound of homicidal
supply side economics.
She pawed wildly
at the pretty yellow blouse,
but the oozing tide
of walmortality pushed
her far out to sea,
well into Sporting Goods,
where a stiff undertow
pulled her back down,
down and under.
Kicked, stomped and bruised,
she managed a weak gulp
of air before submerging
once more in the white trash
miasma. The violent, unrelenting,
shrieking, body-blocking current
flung her serendipitously
toward the shore of Toys,
due east of Infants and Toddlers.
She rested briefly on a dune
of Beanie Babies.
"Forty percent off,"
she gasped uselessly
to the little mannequin.

Search and Rescue
and divine intervention
found the wounded
bargainfishing seafarer
clinging to a gaudy
Snowmobile Barbie display.

The sea drained.

Paramedics carried the survivor,
bruised and gurneyed,
through the glass portal of Hell
where she once again
weakly waved
at the siren's shoal:
"My blouse!"

Bellingham

Bare trees ring the edge
of the little berg on the bay;
Winter settle here,
the little city sleeps
day and night; no bustle
guides traffic; folks amble,
folks mosey. Lights
of industry sparkle
without burning in the distance,
a reminder of the cityhood,
a reminder of commerce.
The bay pushes gently at the shores.

On the cliff where I sit,
hungry eagle hangs on a breeze
above my head, floats along
the line separating sand and sea,
patrolling in vigilant silence.

The little city on the bay
found me here seven years ago
watching the same eagle,
appreciating its patience, its freedom.
Understanding human transience
and the illusion of control
I stored in warm packets,
cheap notebooks,
expensive computers.
I stood there then with no words
no ideas no help no love.
Just a need, obscure as the horizon
where gray sky meets gray water.

The little city on the bay
chatted with fate and time
and encouraged me
to sit on the cliff again
and forced me to listen,
to pay attention this time,
pay attention like this eagle.

Railroad Station, Albany, Oregon

Waiting for late trains
and other gifts of time
driving on loud barren plains
of bone-colored concrete,
flying backward through time zones
and offshore flow,
picking up shards of lives
in stuffy buses and smelly cabs,
obnoxiously bland concourses,
rest stops and platforms.

They all leave.
They all left.

They pass through,
always someplace else
the destination,
journeys wasted,
dragging time across
the tracks, losing it in
the jet engine,
invisible freeway exhaust.

They stop savoring moments.
They stopped savoring.

They no longer taste
a languid afternoon
like a lover's wet mouth.

How Poets Live

Crumpled wad of notepad
curled at my desk:
I sit, I listen.
Banter swirling in the stale air
like a dust devil on a hot day.
A husband needs a pair of jeans:
501s, shrink-to-fit.
And the conference calls begin.
Microsoft error messages,
offering a dissonant Muzak symphony,
personal prohibited phone fun,
spouses lovers friends trusters
party plans reservations
complaints weather reports, and
"No! With who?!"

Concentration long ago
lost hope lost cause lost money,
I sit among them
distinctly outside, distinctly apart
distinctly odd, right in the middle -
the senile, mute grampa
in the middle of all the Christmas fun -
a keyboard-whacking pan of glass,
no sound no smell no taste
crumpled up pain in the ass,
just no business in this business.
Smile and nod, fit in,
melt into the gray fabric
of the little industrial walls
as much as humanly paperly possible.
No bad people here,
no awful trolls, no demons.
Salt of the earth
in sterile short walled cubes.

Sounds wind down
lunch disperses them
like onrushing traffic disperses
crows from old roadkill.

Crumpled wad hovers
above the recycle bin,
awestruck by the persistent
thrumming of dollars in motion.

Scale Model

A scale model of me, they say;
I regard this little boy:
The spherical head
 the wild eyebrows,
 the yogic concentration
on a scoop of chocolate ice cream,
pure enough to shame Buddha;
the insane giggle, the wiggle
when relentlessly properly tickled
and the requisite
Face of the Deeply Offended
 when forced to clean the room:
the inexplicable gentleness
when holding the rabbit,
the rummy incoherence in the morning,
dandelion fuzz-head hair.
everywhere, bleary-eyed,
reaching for cereal, pouring
without opening, cackling
at his own comedy.
I regard this little boy
I sit with him in a big chair,
quietly sometimes,
 with everyone else still asleep
 glad to see him now
all of him, his many personas,
 moods and attitudes
We sit and sit
 and he fidgets and pokes
a finger in my armpit
and I hope someday
he breaks all his silences this way
                    1/12/04 (Kent/Home)

Park Bench, Winter

The camera panned across
a small city park,
but I paused on the dross
of the bench, fairly stark.
Unassuming unpopulated repose
while vapid reporters chattered on
about temps plunging, homeless needing clothes,
then abruptly humping segments: Closeup: Pylon.

Strangely enough, winter in the city
miraculously happened last year, too,
and life on that bench became death unpretty,
too insignificant now to bother you.

On the commercials now, your tiny attention span
(the news producers know your mind)
but the bleak bench hovers in a vision-brand
banging there like the kind
of shadow of a too-bright light,
lingering, burned into my mind,
too involved to put up much of a fight:

Thirteen below then, with no room at the shelter,
Old Talkin' Moe assumed residence
on the recycled plastic bench, with his welter
of gathered garb: old Sonics jacket, incontinence,
tattered blanket, partial sleeping bag, jot of sanity.
Dusk approached, and as the commuters scattered,
cockroach-like, barely passing for humanity.

Talkin' Moe hunkered down with demons and coats,
and when he challenged the demons, the nest shattered
like the quart of Olde English and the last wild oats.
He surrendered at eight, solid by ten,
a little too late for the squad car rolling by,
the first of the Cold Patrols or the mission men.

The officers resorted to hot water to pry
him away from the plastic to keep him intact.
His real name age family loves lives
or how to properly dispose of him remains inexact.

An inch of space in a daily paper:
An entire life's work explained away.
The smarmy news circus returns, the shaper
of public conscience. The bench remains today.

What Happened

The still life of a little boy
with rich, cocoa-brown face,
glittering smile, deep embrace
of life belied the old white
noseless woman on the bar's
big-screen TV.
The grunting, foul-smelling
old men in flannel shirts
hunched over beer and burden
hardly offer a second glance.
"Goddamn pedophile," the slur.
"Just sick sick sick."
The image vanishes
from their consciousness as fast
as the image appears and fades
on the TV behind the bar.
But it remains at large
in the makeovers, gastric bypasses,
nips here tucks there,
faces lives asses psyches altered,
some great societal Want
never discouraged, but fed, scooped
down the gullet by the invincible
omnipotent ABCBFoxNNNetwork
marketing focus groups, by eye
candy vendors and hookers doubling
as pitchmen and ad reps.

The pedophile freak remains
at large and we afford shelter,
havens of dollars and idle worship,
and like a deranged mass of lemmings
we turn on him, repulsed
by the odd little god
we created a few short years ago.
He build a palace we willingly

furnished: now we wish we hope
he imprisons entombs himself
for all eternity, sans syndication.
Mass consumption, assumption,
we confine the divine,
we eat the gods we birth.

Parable for the Perpetually Puckered

Mistakes gathered at the corners
like clusters of schoolkids
finally blocking the path
of the aimless little life
until it absorbed a bit of gumption
from the divine benign cosmos.

The little mistakes saw bits
of determination in the life's lap,
and smeared on its wrinkled shirt.
With plenty of room to spare,
they moved in and made messes
everywhere. Some big, some small.
The life, angered by the messes,
sputtered and fumed and stomped
out some of the mistakes
like little grassfires.
Tired, the life slept.

More mistakes formed in the creases
and folds of the life's thick shirt.
They frolicked. They cavorted.
The life awoke and rubbed its vision.
It saw the mistakes differently.
It formed a bulb of curiosity
and saw it spout crazily,
watching the mistakes like a
big ant farm, or a crazy goldfish.

Gradually and with great care,
the life surrounded the mistakes
gently, with thoughts
and educated guesses
and a few crazy risks
just to irritate the mean,
stuffy old Left Brain.
The life began to relax

with the mistakes woven
into the shirt, and smiled,
all the wiser.

Ocean Shores

I run to the ocean
I try to get away
I run to the surf
I hope to escape
I dream of the quiet
I only hear the roar
I wander along the edge
I let waves lick at my feet
I hope the roaring stops
I hope my head shuts up.

I run to the waves
I wander in the rain
I sprint from my own noise
I know my voices deafen
I need the sea's silent roar
I fall on the sand, breathless
I taste salt, sand, and wind
I begin to breathe
I begin to see gray sky silver sea
I smell great masses of kelp
I hear gulls shriek over crab corpse.

I run to the white crests
I hope for peace
I need peace in my own head
I hear too much roar
I see distraction, nemesis, everywhere.

I know the world chases silence
I see how the loud ones die
I wonder if quiet exists
I fall to my knees in the gray muck
I give up
I surrender to the empty beach
I stand in shiny wet sand

I walk away slowly
I walk forever on this wet sheen
I walk and my footprints disappear
I turn around and understand
I finally see silence.

Not a Pretty Picture

A solitary life with mass appeal:
I look to find the adoring throngs
nowhere in sight, everywhere in my head.
As if America suddenly embraces
eggheaded poets who write with pens.
As if Oprah might smile fondly on my career.
Which, right now, consists of:
Underwear, writing at a tiny table in a hotel,
yes underwear, sweatshirt, and a fountain pen.
A poet, in all the glory a white butt musters;
underwear, fountain pen, cheap notebook.
Cold pizza, yes, the underwear, white legs.
Not just white: Milk, snow dandruff.
I imagine greater things, a greater life
than the pretense of this fountain pen.

Yes, yes, the underwear. The notebook.
I like the pen and the underwear.
I search for rich words worthy of the pen,
and the underwear dares not chafe.
The white snow mild dandruff legs -
but the underwear: Black.
In debt up to my nethers, I dream I write
I prophesy living in circles of importance.
The pen writes well, an excellent tool.
I fail the poetic affectation test.
Not expensive, not ostentatious; just a pen,
a pen that writes well with its
owner bedecked in a pasty white ass.

The pen, the notebook, the ass,
a sweatshirt to preside over the spectacle.
This peculiar spectacle of solitude,
the pen glides past, sits in no judgment,
and the poet longs to rid himself
of the stigma of profundity all poets carry,

certainly not with stumpy white milk legs.
The fountain pen, the underwear, the pizza,
the poet's goosebump milky snow leg dandruff.
Greater than this, surely as debt encroaches,
the pizza causes unquenchable thirst,
far more than necessary, the underwear
the underwear dares not chafe.

Tap water no affectation good reliable penetrates
the chlorine saturated tap water,
and finally with no affection no hope
the poet, the hideous beast dandruff milk,
the poet succumbs to a fatal, lethal.
Oh, the goddamn underwear again, yes, black
the poet succumbs at long last, hideous
mass life with solitary appeal,
he fades away, succumbs most mercifully
to a fatal blow of mundanity.

Lapse in Judgment

My apologies, Mr. Vonnegut:
I still hear your words, my only
living commandment not to let
"literature disappear up its own asshole."
I resisted until now.
I fought it off.
I refused to write about writing,
writers, or overt analysis
of this or that style or genre.
I avoided, skirted the issue.
Until today.
Today, I suck.
To use another word
invites even more pretense
than the tackiness of this slang.
Today, I suck.
Because today I sat
with many other writers and I saw
myself all over the place,
like ransom note letters,
little bits of cliché confetti
all over the place. We talk
publishers and markets and voice
and showing not telling and no
run-ons and passive voice this
and strong openings that and grab
their attention right now because -

I really need a beating.
I whine and whimper
pathetic misunderstood poet
all alone with thousands of others
a poor tortured life
even with these wondrously
turned phrases and nuances -

My god, Kurt. Today, I suck.
I broke my own vow.
I contributed to the miasma
of effete, ivory tower writing.
I not only wrote about them,
I wrote about *me*.

Tomorrow, strength returns.
Tomorrow, fresh ideas emerge.
New topics, new directions, no writers.
As soon as the misery subsides.

Old Song

An old song,
a meandering,
flowery, feminine
old song, played
in jewelry store jingles
at Christmastime,
a weak melody,
somniferous, almost,
but a perfect sentiment
for what you bring
to my life, my love:
You encourage me, never berate;
You prod me, never nag;
You coax me, never drag;
You speak thoughtfully, never prattle.
And you love me,
Never hoping for my
Mutation into Mr. Right.
The old song, mild song,
Long nostalgic song
Still holds for me:
I love How You Love Me.

Homage to Catatonia

I get on at milepost 254 southbound
And the stupor stays until 236.
Twenty minutes a day
In Splendid Catatonia.
I get off at 183, not much better.
Not light yet, not for another half hour.
Lucky for 24-7 access to this workbox.
Otherwise, a bad attitude creeps in.

Primaries and Caucuses

They whirl and wrangle
in public arena,
they kiss babies
they shake hands
until their own crack and chafe.
They travel the country,
crisscrossing it like plodding
gadflies in 757s and obnoxious buses.

They repeat the same set of speeches
until their own eyes
glass over, no longer believing
what their own voices transmit,
transmute, transpose, transdict.
They zoom from place to place,
hoping we promote them
to yet another lofty office,
so they afford to disappear forever,
and run your state your town
your house by remote control.

They probably cared once.
They probably believed what they said.
They probably promised and delivered.
We played along; we play along still,
on the off chance we pick the right one,
the chance to blunt our own cynicism,
to believe for even a second:
This one makes a difference.

We furtively but intently
watch those pretty reporters
freeze in Iowa and New Hampshire,
we hope Our Guy wins
(Quietly, nobody looking),
and return to the callous,

acceptable, blasé' indifference
when CBS projects the wrong winner.
We grind out another candidate.
Four more years.

Modern English

They sit, rapt, in front
of the Energy Star-Compliant
glowing monitor of the Future,
electron guns beaming them
disposable information, spewing
at them words composed
with plastic and metal,
ones and zeros.

He sits, lost in thought,
a pen poised in his hand,
a pen crafted decades ago
in a former life, it waits
beautifully above the thick
paper, for a thought's essence
to trickle from soul to linen
through this conduit.

They remain eight feet apart,
scarcely able to comprehend
the other's' world, though
from time to time one raises
an eye from monitor or nib
long enough to marvel
at the others' ability to dwell there.
A pause of recognition,
connection, perhaps; perhaps distaste.
Worlds apart, they share the words
with different tools, different times.

Real Estate

The search for silence
continues in rural enclaves
and five-acre parcels
where we glimpse
deer and cougar,
coyote and grouse
under the rosy illusion
of quiet, we seek remoteness,
understanding nothing of history
of creation, of plight,
of what harmony means
beyond music. Even these
regulated places remain scarce.
Even artificial solitude
requires perseverance, effort.

I trudge to the middle
of a snow-covered meadow,
strange bit of cold
in the Northwest air, trying
profoundly, desperately to frame
this bit of land in the vision
of a Nooksack, Lummi, Squalicum.
I let my feet, in big Timberland boots,
crunch through the thin white crust.
Great boots, they fail as moccasins,
I fail as Native American,
even in pathetic daydream.
I reek of Hallmark caricature.
Fighting it all back,
warding off historical guilt,
inconvenient pathos,
I take a mental snapshot of the real estate sign,
hoping I live here soon,
while I remember what it looks like.

Carol's Song

Sing your song, little girl,
Tell your story.
Gentle coastal zephyr
Plays with your hair;
Wildflowers tickle your ankles,
Revel in the salt air
And honeysuckle smells.
Your world, your time, your play.
Sing the day away, little girl:
Pure joy, pure joy.

Take a stand, strong woman,
Bare your soul.
Prepare for the journey:
Wool blankets, wild guesses,
Caviar, and invitations.
Sun on your softly crafted face
Carves and caresses, strokes and sears,
And you taste all those years,
Swiss chocolate, wine and rye
Your time, your life, your soul.
Let 'em know right now, strong woman.
Show yourself. Show yourself!

Relax now, old lady,
Time to rest.
You created a world.
Filled it with kids who love you,
And a warm gentleman who brings
Iced tea tonight, and gently
Calls you his wife,
The way he called you wife
A million years ago,
A million years from now.
Your love, your heart, your time
The universe needs that song, old lady.
Sing it sweet. Sing it sweet.

Next Exit

Thread of life, interrupted,
weaving through small towns
connecting big cities
yearning for open sea -
Atlantic, Pacific, Puget Sound,
Lake Winnipesaukee,
Lake Washington and Union
Seattle and Somersworth
so young, so old
fevered wanderlust
and the need to root:
All in me, the Catalyst.
I stitch the world together
in front of me, tapestry
of thought and time,
brown haze, azure hills
catch basins and wild streams
abhorrent timing of love and lust
dwell in me, the Catalyst.
The thread of a life, interrupted,
for now, anyway, recording
the time and the mood
and the soul of the world.

Executive Tech Support

I work with machines some smart people fear.
I get them to behave.
I cajole little idiot boxes
For big warm idiot people
To buy processed food
And live in a compartment
That sprung together in a week
Like my son's Legos.
I tell them not to worry.
I tell them a fix exists.
I calm them down
So they can push the little
Idiot box in the right direction.
I dream of creative things while rebooting.
I dream of writing and living and thinking
And acting like a sane human being.
I dream of Being . . .
I wonder what they dream about
Behind those dim vacant eyes.
The job title imposes a certain largeness,
But the soul they own: How small.
Feeling no better or worse
For either of us, I send the little idiot box
On its new Path of Righteousness
Until the big warm idiot
Screws it up again.

Into Place

Monolithic stones,
Immeasurable mass:
Sinewy efforts
Of burly Egyptians
Or stoic Druids
To complete the pattern,
Erect the obelisk,
Honor the pharaoh.
Monuments of truth,
Homage to passion and calm

The stout little fellow
Drives a shoulder
Into the largest
And smallest boulder,
Thinking insanely:
"Change! Move, damn you!"
Rocks, dusty, in a heap.
Pattern incomplete.
Chaos, vocations, callings, love.
Levers snap. Rollers crush.
"Hmm. Try this, Bubba."
The pleasant waft
Of a feminine drawl
Consternates Mr. Neanderthal.
But a gentle smack here
A careful poke there,
And to follow,
A hug and a wink.
Perhaps some quiet
While Mr. Thickbrow thinks,
As the stones glide into place—
The warmth of a hearth
In his chest--he hears,
"Steps, old son. *Steps.*"

Prehistoric House of Mirrors

A million years ago
I looked at you
And by god you scared me.
Your studied elegance
And stealthy confidence
Shone in the depth of your eyes.
Impenetrable.

I saw my own fear
As I praised your features
And surmised your stature,
And donated a large, chiseled mate.
I shrank as you grew in importance
Confounding my head that knew better.
A million years ago. But somehow,
Your voice surprised me in its richness.
Your words jostled me in their warmth.
About a week ago I looked at you
And my vision unraveled
And I saw your beauty
And I reached you somehow
And I knew, as I know,
As I concentrate,
As I am and as I feel,
I give this to you,
And you understand.

Happy Birthday, Old Man

How ya doin'?
It's been ten years, you know.
Your advice was unintelligible,
But your love was pretty clear.
You knew I don't believe in God.
I knew you didn't, either, long before you did.
You needed the ritual, the structure.
I needed more.
We're still too much alike, you know.
I have my hiding places, just like you did.
I don't drink, though. I can't tolerate being drunk.
Don't smoke, either. But I do like coffee.
And my emotional cubbies and closets.
I remember your pilgrimage to see me. It was brave.
So out of your element, so far from anything resembling home.
Too much for a kid born on a kitchen table on Fremont Street
In Somersworth, New Hampshire.
You went back. I stayed.
I remember the last conversation we had.
You upbraided me for marching against the Gulf War.
You were a Korean War vet after all.
I just didn't know any better. You couldn't tell me
Why I should have been ashamed, just that I should have.
I get like that sometimes, you know.
A ball of fire in my chest, and not a damn word for it.
Writer and all.
All this language is just useless sometimes.
But you knew that, long before I did.
When I got the call ten years ago
It hurt like hell. I thought you had arrived.
I thought you had just about figured it out.
You had overcome so much and gained so little.
I hoped for you. I felt for you. We were so damn alike.
I wonder what the hell you would have thought about that funeral.
The bizarre Hail Mary session over your corpse.
The tin soldier salute in St. Martin's.

Two VFW members handing your ex-wife an American Flag.
You didn't want that war, but you fought it.
You didn't want that life, but you fought it.
You didn't want that marriage, but you fought it.
For me and my siblings. For god and country. You fought it,
Right to your grave. Never asked anything.
Never questioned the orders.
You knew yourself better than you thought.
Always said you were tough.
Damn right you were, old man.
Damn right you were.

Merge Right

A long time ago,
A crusty New Englander
Rode the rails across the country.
He waited. Worked. Subsisted.
Faded from blue to gray and back.
Jumped from panic to infatuation.
Rode his bike too much. Hid.

A long time ago,
A tender Northwesterner
Wrested herself from a life of another.
She waited. Worked. Subsisted.
Hid her dreams in death and children.
Crafted lust a cunning tool.
Indulged in a tattoo. Hid.

Not that long ago,
Two careful, imperfect strangers
Merged on the same path
In an urban maze of impossibility,
And while dancing, eyes darting,
Words failing, silence breaking,
In a brilliant and brief
Flash of Seattle sun,
They ignored the city's madness
And incessant hum of commerce,
And listened to a soft duet of eternity.

A long time from now,
Above the hiss and roar of I-5,
Hawks, gulls and eagles
Share the song, carry it far,
Past capitalism and concrete,
Past buses and buildings,
Into the night, the day,
The sky and the sea,

Where it belongs, my love,
Where it remains forever.

Invisibility

Somewhere in the great machine,
in the red stapler jungle,
in the big clean Steelcase maze,
in the two-panel cube with the half-height wall,
in the nebulous position
in the nebulous department--
Somewhere among the right-wing claptrap
among the new-carpet smells
among the afternoon break popcorn
among the eons of casual Fridays
among the decimation of American souls,
among the mandated cheers of joy and oneness--
Somewhere around the self-important marketeers,
around the encouraged mediocrity
around the carrots and sticks and stolen time,
around the hour hand the minute hand
around the snarling slow commute
around the shiny conference table--
Right next to the perky no-life executive,
next to the killer vending machine,
next to the frontline piece of meat,
next to the walking harrassment suit,
next to the 90-day probation period,
Patience...patience--look!
Reflecting, transmitting,
right through him,
Clear glass or big mirror,
The Invisible Man thrives here, everywhere.

Across the Border

Possibilities
Sparkle on the surface
Of Vancouver's waterways:
Sometimes giddy.
Sometimes elusive
Always bright
Always hopeful
Familiar climate,
Different culture
You show up in places
I never knew
I always knew.

—TD 9/13/00

Freeway, Claws, Christmas

I-5 drives,
Bellingham and Everett,
Mountlake Terrace and Kent
The distance of intimacy,
The shortest between two points;
Christmas scratches at my door again,
Like that stray, horny, cross-eyed cat
I struggle to ignore or feed.
I let it in this year.
I opened the door.

It purrs. Lovingly smashes
Its bulbous head on my shins.
Yowls through commercials
And lights and truly awful
Renditions of "Jingle Bells."
Bumps into my chairs
And annoys me into loving it.
I relent.
I let it in this year.
I open the door.

It hops into my lap,
Claws dangerously close
To Paydirt. It knits those talons
Into my thighs and jeans.
I wince, but it settles in. Warm.
Quiet. It purrs.
Soon, two blond kids will pierce this peace
For a louder one, their shrieks,
Smiles and gifts filling my apartment
And my soul, diving into Christmas
Like the end of a waterslide.
I let them in, of course.
I open the door.

I hug them quickly
And bury my face in their hair
To hide my tears, not sure
If they understand "happy crying"
Or how lots of driving
Means lots of thinking,
Or how a cockeyed, unneutered hairball
Dropped Christmas in my lap one year.

Elixir

Sensual bitter fragrance
Enchants a Seattle suburb crowd.
They pay absurd sums
To keep it alive, make it hum,
A fast, hours-long guitar solo
In the nervous system.
Jack you up and launch you
In your Lexus SUV,
That rolling oxymoron of the Eastside,
Headache preventer, thought accelerator,
Galvanizer of neo-urban culture:
They worship you with fat wallets,
As clerics distribute the Host
In your early morning fog,
Blessing you through the first
Two-hour traffic jam du jour
And the Venti two percent quad
Mocha no-whip makes a lovely
Powerprop in that first meeting.
Drink your culture, baby, while it's still hot.

Dear Miss Twenty

I hear you in autumn wind
And the voice that drives me to my knees;

I see your mosaic in women I know
Or thousands I wish for;

I smell your scent, tuned to the rhythm of heels on concrete,
Or the leather of a good hiking boot on rock and root
As both fade into the silent sky.

I taste the mint of your mouth as consciousness flutters,
Or the harsh bite of an average red wine on your cautious lips;
Both leaving me breathless, either leaving me senseless

Mr. Idiot Romantic still lives, I see,
But the horny teenager grew up.

Miss Twenty, I graduated. I paid my loans.
I majored in Poor Judgement. Scored my MFA in Victim.
No interest in the Dating Fiasco. I learned, Miss Twenty.
Oh yes: I learned.
Now please come home.

Mother's Day

Between toothaches
And tummyaches
Among tears and travails
Winding through
The inexplicable responses
Of five-year-old logic,
Of ten-year-old behavior:
"Nope. I didn't break that."
"Don't spank me, I'm cute!"
"You made me spill it!"
"Monsters ALWAYS mess up my room."
Some words describe you:
Patient. Constant. Forever.
You guide them to responsibility
Shepherd them to honesty
Listen to their meandering stories
As they steady themselves, unknowing,
Leaning too hard or not enough
On their rock, their foundation
Munching cookies, sipping rootbeer,
Making messes, pictures, expressions -
Unconscious, honest love for you -
Every minute of today and forever
Into their teens, twenties, eighties
Rearing their own, sending them
On their way until they finally, fully
Understand the roots of "Mother."
And begin again.

Truckmaters

The tomatoes nobody planted
grow copiously under my truck
and all the carrots in tidy rows
in the rich fertile soil in the
railroad tie bordered, staked and roped
clearly marked and fenced garden
in our verdant backyard paradise
conspicuously avoided our atmosphere.
The perfectly round, uncannily red fruit
never sees a bed of greens in a salad,
downed furtively before reaching the kitchen,
like a teenager sneaking porn in the dark.
A fruit, not a vegetable. Remember that.
Nothing this good sounds like "vegetable."
And it grows happily, ignored all year,
under my truck, blithely stretched across
the hostile juniper and heather.
Little tomatoes bunched like grapes everywhere
unexpected unwanted unplanned.
All the porn I want, right there.
Panic: Now I know they exist. NO!
Responsibility! They'll surely die!
The drama passes quickly, as a fly
alights on my ear. I back the truck out
carefully avoiding a cluster near left front.
More ripe ones to pick later.
I pause in the driveway, looking at the
crazy tomatoes, wondering if they wonder
if this is how I treat
all the luck in my life.

Where I Am Now

When I sit quietly
The symphony begins
Slowly the strings of memory
Come to life and
The vibrations conjure a voice
In ecstasy, in closeness, in union
And as the oboe begins its solo
I hold a warm hand under the eaves
Out of the rain, eyes holding tenderness
Such a pure time, long time ago
And as the tympani shakes my foundation
Turning the pages of distrust and fear,
The raw torment of something beautiful
Dying hopelessly helplessly, swiftly,
Tears wash into the present and the violins
Cry, too. The piano cradles the psyche and my
Eyes open to a new soul, brave soul,
No remorse or regret, just present.
The sun ends the symphony
And I sit and watch the sea
Relentlessly carving a new world.

Untitled Poems

Yeah, I notice you.

Everything fits perfectly
You visually reek of sex
Yeah, I want you.
Your gestures hit their marks
Your hips: My god.
Yeah, I need you
I think of your mouth
And I get dizzy
Yeah, I'm petrified
Damn right I run away.

9/12/99

She sits there, you know,

Hair like a whitewashed tumbleweed,
Headset on, taking the call like a pro,
The way only she can for nine bucks an hour
Big Brother knows when she goes to the bathroom,
When she takes a break
Decides to eat lunch (she might nibble a bit of bagel
if it's a carbo day),
Waxes surly with a customer—
So she toes the line and swallows the attitude
And everybody buys it
everybody loves it
And all the while
Everybody hates it
Everybody knows better
'Cause if the Machine stops,
Everybody dies. Or survives. Same thing.

9/13/99

The lunch couple nukes their

frozen sodium bombs together
in something resembling wedded bliss:
The vague awkwardness
as they try to veer
from the amused glances
of other work-related inmates.
I hope happiness awaits them,
embraces them as it should.
They deserve it, frumpy though they may be.
We all deserve it, cynical as we are.
Some day, some time when the world
won't hold us all,
we'll envy them,
we who needed solitude.

9/13/99

Waiting for a green from Fort Worth

Sitting on three thousand horses,
Looking at orders and USA Today,
The day unfolding
Six thousand horses trailing,
Four thousand tons after that
Pedestrians amble by, pausing
In awe of all that power
Wheels of commerce
Wheels of trade
Keep it moving
Keep it profitable
He sleeps alternating twelves
As money thumbs its nose
At Circadian Rhythms
Steel wheels, steel rails
Big and bulky
Fast and stealthy
America tolerates and reveres
And denies its addiction to
These rolling power plants.
Seeing his green, he lays his paper aside:
A staccato bell awakens,
The hum from idle rises,
The whole thing suddenly moves.
A horn echoes off any available surface.
Here I come.

9/18/99

How do you stand it?

You talk of flying to Maui.
Place you stay.
Setting up friends with well-heeled men
and exploring "cute" little towns
with the same effortless swipe
of a fork on a fresh croissant.

How do you do it?
Do you believe your own pretense?
Do you really bask in your superiority?
Is it just a shell?
Where is your animal?
Your delicate voice into that phone demands I listen and wonder.
So smooth
yet the voice rasps on my eardurm
with societal persistence.
What passions arouse you outside
of lining up the next client
or pleasing a boss?
How it must feel . . .
Or does it?

10/18/99

Icy dull staccato winter

Dragging through my soul
As the rain begs for my attention
I want to run naked through
The storm but so many eyes
So many people . . . .
I crave the anonymity of dark and distance
And I succeed masterfully:
Nobody knows me. No one.
Who tries to be alone,
Who seeks the shadows at every turn,
Who craves the dark and quiet?
 "We" or just "I"? Because I long
For your touch, I need your body
As you desire mine, but tonight,
Chasms and eons apart,
You and I starve silently again,
Waiting for ridiculous odds to drag us
Mercilessly into the light
And cling to each other in our madness.

11/16/99

Crept ahead slowly

Rising from the mire
Old lovers and perception
Compost for the living
The primal need to share and mate
Eludes technology and time
I know as I heal
I want that again—
Those touches, the caresses,
The way the passion burns;
The heat of spontaneity and lust.
But also:
Reading the Sunday paper
In a square of sunlight
Your lap as a pillow.
I read "Travel"
You read headlines.
A pair of cats on the couch.

3/11/00

Your hand on my face

Told the story:
It seared my skin. I staggered.
To feel you that close
Without kissing,
Without attempting,
Without a long, probing look
Told the story:
Not yet. Not now. Not right.
One night we exchanged
Furtive goodbyes in a parking lot
And you kissed my neck lightly
Once again, forced to assume innocence
As my pulse raced
As my head swam,
But we told the story again:
You love HIM. You live THERE.
Weeks pass. Months pass. Years.
We cling to the story
And its wondrous safety.
You know how my hands feel,
How my mouth tastes,
Where my tongue travels.
You know the story.
Your story.
I write my own.

3/12/00

Linear humans start and stop.

We end. Cosmic blink.
Lifetimes fit between
Eyelid up and eyelid down
Matters of scale and proportion
Magnified between our ears
And we continue along
An immortal path:
We consume ourselves,
Our world, like cheap
Flavorless gum.
We exalt nothing but ourselves
And rejoice in our own myth.

4/5/00

I hold that little red shirt,

That tiny fleece gateway
To a quickly receding lifetime,
I see it on a little blond boy
With big brown eyes, kicking
A soccer ball half his size,
Not knowing Daddy leaves
Tomorrow and stays away.
I see it on the boy, that perfect
Boy as I toss him like a toy
Flipping skyward, guttural giggling
Spilling out of him onto me
The shirt lives with me and I
Watch it as I hear kids giggle
Outside my apartment.
Some days I just smile at that shirt.
Some days I wipe my eyes with that shirt.

4/5/00

So many pieces:

Two little blond kids,
An apartment and a house
Eighty miles of freeway
Seven years of guarding
Against failure, raw emotion,
And the ugliness
Of togetherness.
We signed in, smiling,
We signed out, shaking heads.
Ink on paper either way,
No stopping either way.
Today the Clerk and I
Stamped somber documents
With somber names
So all could see
Individuals again, instead
Of that dead couple
With the two beautiful kids
In the old minivan.
An announcement in the newspaper,
Writing our names a few more times
Completes the officialness
Such a prolonged and ugly death
Of something once beautiful.

4/18/00

I fit somewhere, I suppose

But not here, not now
Too many memories, most bad.

I belong somewhere, I guess
But not there, too close
That little city killed me once. Never again.

Someone loves me somewhere, I think.
But not like this, not just me.
My best foot aches in the forward position.

I see happiness, I hope.
Hazy behind those hills—a few miles more
Thin blanket of Tomorrow nearly keeps me warm.

4/18/00

All right, damn you, look at me.

No spring chicken.
Few pounds over the border.
Always a half-hour early
Snore like a freight train.
Hate opera, love baseball,
Tall as a fire hydrant.
Headless chicken crazy.

Now hold my hand
And jump.

4/18/00

Do you see the value,

Pouring confusion and anxiety
Into a cheap, innocent notebook,
Chasing your own insecurities
Like a dumb mongrel dog?

Drive the demons from the recesses
Of the soul with the unlikely weapon.
Soothe yourself with
Your own point of view
Your own righteousness:
Live and die by the pen.

Write away the foibles and fears
None of that messy human
Interaction. Run quietly
Through the world, nonstop.

That hand on your shoulder
That fixed gaze you noticed,
That crazy phrase she said—
It all matters, it all fits,
It all resides away from the pen.

4/22/00

Quiet; solace evades the loud.

Stealth impressions of a life.
I watch and wait.

Slow; nothing worthwhile speeds by.
She pushes the auburn strands behind her ear.
I find it erotic.

Sure; furtive gestures die quickly.
Bluffing, wild guessing conversation.
I lock her eyes and shut up.

The dream empties into the bright
Warmth of the early morning,
The faint aftertaste
Of sensuous chocolate,
The savory sluggishness of good massage,
The idiotic grin of lost teen lust.

I dress, sip coffee.
Read the morning paper.
Another Saturday in the Complex.
Another day of my life
Taking aim at yours.

5/13/00

Not enough

To say the words
And act the part
It must flow through you,
Through me.
Blood through an athletic physique
Breathe your soul into mine
And write lousy poetry like this
And see wonder in my eyes
Try to feel the breath of night
And the cold full moon
Searing your taut perfect skin
As a summer washes over you
And laps at my feet,
Binding us in silent unison
To earth, sky, and ocean.

6/11/00

Sun cools the water

In a small town up North
And the moving van growls
Into the neighborhood
Salty smells and roses
Almost mask the sound of the train
Which almost obscures
The old voices in my head
"Just stay in one place.
Just once."
The little helpers carry little boxes
And stake out little territories:
"My wall! My corner!"
While curious eyes peek over hedges
As I hope I fit,
Hope I stay,
Wonder anew at this life of mine
And who will love,
Who will fit
In the apartment
Next to the sea,
The park, and the tracks.

7/10/00

Since the Time of Awareness,

Attempts at reason failed,
Scrawled on papyrus
Or clacked on a keyboard,
Meaning drives the medium
Whether it asks or tells.
I live I love I mate I hate I die
Not much difference in us humans
Connecting those dots—the art
Of the Writer, Painter, Sculptor, Thinker—
Yes: That causes Life
Shaking the meaning out of life
Like a wolf kills a rabbit.
Let that drive you.
You live.

8/27/00

The images burn:

Those hands, caressed by water,
Caressed by soft light over the sink
Forced desire back through my throat
Far enough to hear myself offer tea
But I wonder at their passion; still
Poised there, shining, glowing, ready
For face, chest, back, shoulder
Dripping power, vibrant sensuality.

And you sat at the other end
Of the couch and my heart stopped again:
The unexpected glory of poor lighting
Delivered composition of the Masters:
Your small, finely-boned face
Catching just enough color,
Just enough shadow, just enough enigma
To make me stammer and lose
What tenuous grasp I borrowed
On your words. Your eyes
Pierced room's shadow,
My shadow, the night, the moment
And suddenly you left
And suddenly, I still smiled.

9/5/00

Labor Day for the masses,

But you carry the shrapnel
Of years in your soul,
Even the blonde-haired beauty
And innocence of your children
Reminds you of potential and tragedy.
I know today lives differently for you,
Pretty Lady, I know.
Never knowing the whys,
Looking past the hows
Staring into the somedays.
But today starts now.
You live and you love.
You. All you.
Let autumn remind you
Forever of the crispness
Of the morning and the scent
Of fir boughs, the brilliant
Variegated twilight, the giggling
Kids running through leaves,
The gentle bite of a good hard cider,
And the warmth of a life of love
You created.
Celebrate your life, Pretty Lady.
I promise you, everyone will.

9/5/00

Long before you drove

Your SUV to Costco,
You rode rickety rails into town
To talk and shop and stock up.
You braved coal cinders and cold cars
Or you rode warm, clean and dry
On a train with a name:
Southern Crescent. Empire Builder.
City of New Orleans.
You waited in hallowed
Transportation cathedrals
Like Grand Central or Penn Station
Or shacks and house-like depots
With names like Easton and Blaine.
You knew the folks there—
Ticket handler, the Express Agent,
Maybe even a conductor or telegrapher.
City to city became a social event
Lined with people to help and guide,
Irritate and obfuscate,
But definitely not isolate.
Long before you roll up the windows
On your forty thousand dollar
Chamber of silence, think
About the steel threads
That you kathump across
On your way to Costco, and how they
Stitched communities together.

9/10/00

I hide from the sun

In a little coffee shop
Sipping time and place
Your words, still
Wedged in my soul,
Tenderness and fear
Shrouding sunlight through
The quaint glass door.
Honestly: Am I ready
Prepared? Waiting?
Oh, hell, no.
The shock and the warmth
Arrived at once,
The same wave.
If you knew how careful
I am with that heart
Of yours, how softly
I tread—Oh,
I think you do.
Poets become silent
Very quickly, you know.

9/12/00

Such a different tone this time

My body listens to me now,
My soul feels the day
Rolling gently, silently northbound
In brilliant sun and blue
Occasional chime of the horn
Seals and Great Blue Herons out there
Quiet travel chatter in here
Flying past coastline and farm—
I bask in this today;
Before, I stewed.
We cross the Stillaguamish,
Skagit, Snohomish Rivers
Twisting through little Nowheres
Shrouded in fog and pop back into
Sunlight, needle diving
Again and again into the tapestry
Of today. I savor
The sounds, the swaying,
The hawks on fences,
The fog caressing the train
The now of my life.

9/13/00

A warm wind carries

Jasmine, honeysuckle and rose
Through the burgeoning dusk,
Well-dressed people stroll
Through the well-dressed garden,
Jaunty topiary monoliths
Preside over the formalities
Of the day with amused stances.

I wait quietly for once.
Appreciate this rose garden,
Revel in the cool evening,
Calm anticipation of your presence
All new territory, new sensation,
As a smile reaches my lips,
I lean toward wonder:
Easy as breathing?
Perhaps.
The roses hear my smile.

9/14/00

Believe in the day:

See it from behind the counter.
Drive the big bus with Cranky Driver.
Walk the downtown beat
With Officer Maligned.
Answer the phone
With Commission-Only Solicitor.
Serve manufactured foodstuffs
With Overworked waiter.
Show kids how to read
With Overlooked Teacher.
Pick at roadkill with Loathsome Crow.
Run from humans with Orphan Dog
Dodge twilight traffic with Frightened Deer.
And know, as you breathe,
As you blink, as tides caress coastlines
And stars explode and fade,
The community of consciousness
Excludes no one.
Believe in the day.

10/8/00

You want so badly

To believe him.
Believe in him
You feel trust well up
Like a shout of triumph.
You beat it back—
It beat you twice before
You frame pictures in your mind
In your heart,
He ran to her, not you.
He fell silent with you, not her
He blew it.
You remain.
In the house, in the bed.
The urge to forgive.
The wound open, raw.
Gallows humor
Permeates your monologues,
But I admire the beauty
And the strength
Of the woman before me—
The powerful eyes and careful mouth—
And I honor the courage
Of the warrior I see
And I feel your desire
To rest in the arms
Of the love you deserve.
Peace now, fragile warrior.
Peace.

10/8/00

The sanctuary we reveal

In our moments of talk,
Moments of silence,
Hours of lovemaking
Finds us everywhere:
When nothing
Or too much
Swirls in my head—
Metal traffic
Mental traffic
Intersections and merges
Annoying honking mundanity
I revel in the sense
Of your touch
And how much sense
We make
Together.

10/21/00

Folded over me,

A velvet glove
Soaked in night's dew,
Still, quiet caresses
And rhythmic dance,
Breath, in whispers,
Touch . . .
Bold, harsh, and sweet,
Scents of rose and cinnamon,
Languorous and lush,
Garden of dusk
Following midnight
To its natural conclusion.
You fit well.
Whole and flush
I dream again,
Silence and voices
Crowd my soul.
I forget
Me.

11/19/00

Steel wheels

On steel rails
Gliding and hoping
Quietly in the night
Stealing away
From the railing city,
Flowing past rivers
Rocking gently
Where the railheads meet,
Where roadbed softens,
Where lovers kiss
Under bridges
Over mountains
Swiftly penetrating
Hills and valleys
A knowing tongue,
A curious mistress.

11/19/00

After the talking stops

And the feeling starts;
After the words fail
And the stomach tightens;
When the freeways surge again
And I still look for answers;
As the world continues
The starkness of Night and Alone
Grows louder,
Growls with the stealth of a cougar,
Howls like a coyote at dawn,
And fills my chest with emptiness,
I know I begin.
I know the journey.
I know.

12/30/00

Elements of lives

Lived thoughtless
And courageous,
Converging like two
Unkempt paths in a sacred
Place of nature,
Nothing but intentional life ahead,
Nothing but accidental joy and fear behind
You look into me sometimes
And sometimes I spew
Sentimental sap like this
You look into me sometimes
And sometimes all my static stops
And sometimes I look into you—
I wonder I question I smile
I shrug I shake my head I see
Your earrings on my nightstand
And marvel at us and how
Deliberately we share our Now.

1/1/01

Packed up my mistakes

And moved south again:
Sunny cold frost-scraping morning
Driving a gas-sucking behemoth
Rolling through Skagit Valley
Thought about the old life
Shook my head over the ex-wife
And the deceptively serene
The commonplace green
Garage's worth of tools and time.

Light streamed into the cab
And the roar of the freeway
Stifled most bad thoughts:
Brisk afternoon thinking of spring
Rolling into the Kent Valley
A big square noisy smelly truck
Full of future and gratitude
Tools, time and love.

I hope I bring it to you.
I hope it grows and smiles.
I hope it kills I-5 miles
As your garage fills
With my life and humble skills
I realize again, right now,
I feel nothing but home.

2/10/01

The time lost, found,

Lives freed and bound
Facing history's ministries
No patience no regard
Silicon and spinning magnets
Elegant castles of air, despair
Money everywhere, nowhere
Worth, meaningless;
Meaning, worthless.
Find it on the bottom line
Meet your targets, deadline
Work, humiliate, die
In shoe boxes of glass
Think outside the box
Live and die in the box
And cover your ass
Another fine Capitalist Moment
Brought to you—
Delivered straight to your door—
By the vacant streamlined
Clean and thoughtless smiling
Corporate whore
Who blew up your mailbox
Last Halloween.
Lock up the food!
God rest ye, merry gentlemen:
Lock up the food,
Lest they figure it all out.

11/3/01

The idiocy of bureaucracy,

The stench of the lunchroom,
The burden of the warden,
The Protector of Paychecks,
The corporate corpses--
All still twitch in the machine.

Meek management,
Corpulent contentment,
Boredom's boardroom,
Unaesthetic antiseptic
Antithetic anesthetic
All still mingle in the machine.

Obtrusive in your silence,
This opulent martyrdom:
They kill slow and steady
They kill completely
They kill innocently
They play marbles with your soul.

Practical and pedantic
Confident and confusing
Accessible and averse
Positive and pathetic
Dumbfounded and diligent
More fodder for the machine.
They play marbles with your soul.

11/27/01

He was old, in the way

Of education and reason
He stood empathetically,
In the way
Of a familiar sage.
His only affluence, knowledge,
In the way of a
Non-tenured, middle-aged professor.
But he held specific sense:
Me, me alone, all.
Not threatening nor ominous,
Not friendly nor jovial,
Yet caring, and lethally honest.
Right between very young
And very old, far away
From innocence or cynicism
Just somebody who knew.
Knew.
His words pierced religion,
Transcended philosophy
And forced a brutal,
Beautiful focus
Of time, thought, and purpose,
A prism taking all the colors
Back to pure white.
He reached in,
Took hold,
And showed me.
I write today because of this.

12/23/01

The noise of the day

The news of the damned
The rhythm of the Proles—

I peaked today.
Saturated.
Accepting no further input.
Off. Shut. Out. Gone.
Talk to the eggplant.
Over wires, through air,
In waves, by discrete signal,
It permeates your being,
Much like Black Lung and the coal miner.

The sound of the day
The news of the dead
The oratory of plastic actors--

Three stories repeated,
Repeated every half hour,
Painful sameness, different voices,
Same sources, different prices,
Disjointed, distended, disembodied;
Death, toothpaste, war, flatulence, maiming--
No matter for these empty-headed
Conduits of informational effluence.
Just turn on the pump.

The static of the day
The news of the dreary
The stench of rotting language.

The halfhearted humor
And idiotic banter
The Platonic NewsCouple
And their smarmy quips
Infiltrate my car, my home, my space.
Auditory macaroni and cheese. AM. FM.
Channel 1,2,3,4,5, six billion.
I lost patience today. I found "Off."
I used it well.

The silence of the day,
The news of the Nothing,
The drive-by, self-inflicted quiet . . .

Sometimes I find myself
Lost in angles in curves in maple
Sometimes I lose myself
Found in cyberspace no reason
Sometimes I lose myself
Finding just the right word time reason
Sometimes I find myself lose myself
Amuse myself lose a season
Sometimes I lose my name
Finding focus on just
One
Thing.
Sometimes I lose my watch my wallet
Finding out the show starts moments ago
Some times I find myself losing days
Finding myself
Sometimes I lose the planet
Finding other worlds right here--
Never fear:
I never lose you.
You travel in my soul.

3/28/02

Subtle aggression

Wending its way toward payoff
Just think this way for us,
Just for a few years,
Then, scram!
Swallow the bait
Think less and less
Bright shiny consuming future
No matter, just sell it, baby
Sell it.
We mock the uniforms
As the water covers
Our nostrils,
Fills our lungs.

2/13/03

In different times,
in a pine-paneled room,

lantern-lit, sandalwood fragrance,
a woman silently appeared
beside the ornately carved bed.
The man watched without movement.
He looked at her purely
for the first time in his life.
The woman, wearing only a blue shawl,
only saw him as well.
Chaos of war and weather
poverty and politics
all rained down on the beautiful house,
but when the shawl fell
he saw her completely again,
heard nothing else,
never let their eyes unmeet,
even as her warmth enveloped him
even as their tongues remained impossibly silent
swallowing words with unconscious hunger.
She met his gaze with uncompromising
abandon, gliding over him
in breathless dance until reckless
sounds of love exploded within them,
her taut breasts finally slowing on his chest.
In different times he knew so much, so little.
In different times, she needed a knight.
They grew old apart.
They lost touch.
In different times
the warmth of the sun
and nothing told with words
represent all a human trusts.

1/28/04

Sitting on the edge

of the low brick wall
sitting on the edge
of her whole being,
the little girl wished.
She wished for her brother
to return from Iraq,
for her parents to stop fighting,
for her President to make sense,
for her classmates to like her.

Sitting on the edge
of the low brick wall
sitting on the edge
of her fragile wonder
she held her breath
and flicked an old nickel
into the shallow, cracked fountain.
She heard nothing
but the steady trickle
of recycled water
and bubbling unrequited hope.

All quiet, all honesty
stays contained
in the pigtailed innocence
sitting on the edge of forever.

1/31/04

The rain pummeled the house

by the river, and it pummeled
one family into submission.
The town pulled together.
They filled sandbags,
toiled tirelessly, shoulder to shoulder
in the peculiar warmth
of late October,
peculiar warmth for the little valley.

They worked together in efficient panic
the bond of desperation
swelling with each wet burlap bag
stuffed, then stacked like a low brick wall.

The family watched their home,
their life until now
slip into the River and disappear,
lost to a hundred year flood.

In town, bakers and bookstore clerks
work and slog and encourage
perfect strangers to help
band together, to form a family
right now to fight this natural foe.

The sweat and the rain mingle;
there exists no difference
they flow together.
Silty water seeps between the bags
as the Skagit crests. They wait.
They breathe and sweat together. They wait.
They wait.

The rescue team finds the family
huddled under a huge oak, weeping
despair filling their sobs.

The river crests; the rain subsides.
The town relaxes. Rejoices briefly.
With the family joining the family
they rest briefly. At dawn, they work.
The family rebuilds the lives, memories
restoring the town forever.

2/4/04

Three thousand of us, packed

into that grand ballroom.
Three thousand, ignoring
Fire Marshall capacity
all standing close enough
to examine skin pores and ear hair
shoulder to rib, big dumb grins
all facing the podium
all awaiting the Candidate.
The heat the noise the anticipation
driving the huddled mass to hysteria.
The anticipation of a subtle but stern
change of direction, administration,
driving us all to scream and cheer.
The whispers of history.
The curious monogram.
The wake of another illegal war.
The stench of corruption
all disappeared that night
at that podium in a Seattle hotel.
Thousands of us, right there.
Thousands of us believed, right there.
We believed in the ability
to change our minds our lives
the course of our country.
Dissent and belief.
Dissent and thought.
Questions and solutions -
Patriotism at its best.

2/6/04

What next?
After you extract
the last drop of crude
from Afghanistan, Iraq,
Texas, Alaska, wherever works,
what follows?
Another Grand Manifest Destiny?
Another Era of Good Feelings?
How then to justify
the millions dead, the species lost?
"Our Great Nation" this,
"With God on our side" that,
The Texas President and his
Worm-tongued entourage
repeat ad nauseam the lies
and misdirections of his
cloistered upbringing
and half-assed education,
the televised culture offering
a willingly purchased backdrop
to soundbites and photo ops.
The P.T. Barnum of our generation,
the time imminent
when the dyslexic presidential appointee
from Crawford, Texas returns
to his oil-soaked roots,
the horizon bodes ill
for fooling all of the people
all of the time.
Read more books, W,   2/8/04
   read more books   Buckys 4th & Meeker

137

Janet Jackson stole the show

halftime diversion for the Patriots
GW in the White House
the Columbia's Anniversary
We captured Saddam
found nothing but oil in Iraq
Karl Rove still runs the country.
Some of us try to break free.
We mass in Iowa, New Hampshire
We pin hopes on a different JFK,
understanding the difference
We remain abroad, we remain domestic,
outsiders in the world we dominate
with our McCulture and McPride
our Hilfiger jeans widescreen TVs
satellite dishes Martha Stewart wishes
and that poor sick Michael Jackson
old man white woman boy lover
reality TV and the smallest
attention spans ever to grace
network news, owned by the Rich
The very rich. The rich and the Right
The very right.
So much to buy to occupy
Networks and cable tell us
what how when to live.
We try to keep up,
So far behind, always behind.

2/8/04

Spring smells breach the small town

despite the calendar's insistence
on the February chronology,
Hallmark-created holiday
blares its way into grocery stores
and smarmy advertising.
The familiar story from home.

Over there, though, a different story:
A small body count, in war terms,
but rising; a deluge of bombings
snipings, accidental deaths
more inane ramblings from politicians
and pundits, more of the same
from local news. We watch. We wait.

Small buds on the maples and elm,
tulips and daffodils in the Skagit Valley
talk of Cactus League baseball
afternoon shadows shrinking
in the globally warming sun
all seems well; all seems normal.
We watch. We wait. We hope.

2/14/04

I stood on the edge of the development

at the edge of where nature
became insufficient somehow;
I took a deep breath, pondering
as I watched a flock of coots
paddle quietly but deliberately
away from us humans,
and I looked to the far shore:
Pillars rose imperceptibly above
the still, dark lake, and I found
myself transported to the era
where those pillars supported
entire trains, entire communities
along that shore, when we humans
found walking invigorating,
and train trips acceptable, I witnessed
the whole economy of that little village
along the shore flourish and vanish
with the railroad
the era the ethic, the very age.
I step back from the edge
wondering if I could live
in such a place. I ponder more,
as the coots slowly return.
Wherever I live
I hope to leave my own
small footprint.
Nothing more.

2/20/04

They stop in the clearing,

unfazed by passing traffic
looking up occasionally
to see who joins the circle.
They trust you implicitly.
The law of the animal,
this innocent doe, grazing
gently at the edge of the new
development, the old farm,
the big valley, the small world,
it disappears behind them,
in front of them, around them;
they concentrate, they sniff,
such good grazing, such
a good grasp of now, and such
good teachers, these quiet animals,
such good instructors
on the finer points of humanity.
Everything they need in front,
behind, all around, then, now,
no difference to them, stepping
slowly, short purpose, wet grass,
sniffing freshly – crushed moss,
causing startled gentle pauses
from bikes, from strollers, from cars,
from obliterated points of view
in the big valley, surrounded by hills
and the treachery of pavement,
the comfort of an overcast afternoon.

3/1/04

My One True Love

cries at sappy movies,
she makes my lunch
and she calls me honey.

My One True Love
giggles at my silly puns
she says she likes my buns
and she snores hard at night.

My One True Love
teaches kids in the daytime
she corrects papers at night
and she smiles at me over tea.

My One True Love
kisses me lots and hugs me
she likes big breakfasts
and she reads the Travel section.

My One Tue Love
likes little furry rabbits,
and big hunky movie stars
She calls me every day.

My One True Love
smiles brighter than any ol' star
she spends her love like stolen money
she gives her heart all the time.

My One True Love
always comes home to me
she says, Hi, Honey
And I know how lucky lucky
I smile and smile and kiss her.

3/1/04

142

I still find it difficult

to think of you in past tense
even after thirteen years.
Your dimpled, smirk, bashful
little smile still shows up
on me now and then.
Even on your grandson.
All of us smile the same way
None of us find words in anger.
Today, for the first time
since your heart stopped
in that little house where I grew up
I cried like a psych patient.
It burst out of me like an alien force.
I thought about you and my son.
Giggling together behind my back.
Playing those bizarre video games
with him, like we used to at his age.
Spoiling him with ease, not money.
You share so much in your lives, you two.
Both nuts. Both admire your own humor.
Then: Nothing. Just an image
of your small plot, wedged
between a chainlink fence
and an access road in the little town
that killed you. My little boy
never met his real grampa. PePere.
I still wonder if this ignorance
really improves his life.

I made that connection today.
I understood why I cried.
Your birthday never meant much to you;
Your grandson loves them.
I used to. See? We all belong together now.
Providence prevents that,
and as I watch the rain
pummel the flowers outside
I really lose control, knowing
how much I missed, how much
that little boy missed, feeling
like two generations
just plain missed.
Not fair. I sob. Not fair.

3/4/04

Two years from now

when the McGuard locks
the last big white door
and over a hundred years of America
evaporates in the silence
of the stilled factory,
when the last of the paychecks
evaporate in the panic
before unemployment;
when the stockholders nod glibly
at the black in the balance sheet;
when the ink flows from Slovenia
out of a Chinese Sheaffer pen;
when the local museum displays
black and white archival photos of 2004;
when the history of a small town in Iowa
evaporates like thin vapors in a fan;
We, the numbers,
We, the people
Encourage you to list your accomplishments:
Happy stockholders
A town's shattered identity
People steeped in squalor,
greed resolute and tall.
An excellent contribution
to the culture of excess.
And please, visit Fort Madison soon:
Vacation in 2006
We extend warm greetings
but bring your own hotel

3/11/04

Nicolas, from Madrid,

wrote to me today.
He says Madrid mourns
and the skies weep for all of Spain.

They rode the train, he writes,
his black ink blotchy with tears.
Just everyday riding the train.
They meant no harm.
Mothers and children.
No policy makers, no presidents,
Why? He asks, hopelessly.
I know so little about these things.
My pen hangs above the page -
Nicolas remains unaware
of the intent on my face,
the pleading, the desire to help -
my pen dries up before
I say anything worthwhile.

Three years ago I felt like him,
incredulous, small, and helpless
and a million other words unfound.
And I know his pain today
still seeing those towers fall
when I blink sometimes.
And I know, Nicolas y Parres,
Spain's strength lies in you.

3/12/04

Sometimes in early spring

before the sun sets on winter
and rises on summer
anticipation builds hope builds
for new life and real beginnings.
Sometimes I feel as if
we deserve a chance, we humans,
we deserve a chance to fix
the messes of our creation,
to stop improving and developing,
scraping the topsoil for strip malls
plowing farms under for Wal-Mart.
But we have a president today
who insists on colonizing the Moon,
Mars, whatever succumbs first.
His hubris floods the airwaves daily,
his ignorance outshone only by arrogance,
a gaudy neon tube, pink,
on a deserted urban street.
His handlers run the country,
some say, the world.
If I believe that, I say:
Let us bomb and plunder ourselves
into the oblivion we deserve;
a thorough job, so we never return.
If we allow an idiot like that
to run anything more than a hot dog stand,
let alone the USA,
we deserve a slow, painful death,
like all the other expendable species
we exterminate every day.

3/23/04

Spring's sullen day with chipper people

banter in the shelter from the drizzle,
traffic lights outside the only color
coffee flows freely indoors
rain drizzles meekly outdoors
people trudge to the entrance
and open up like tulips once inside.

A mix of Jazz and Oldies
filters through polite exchanges
and the squeaks of rubber on tile
and the rustling of Goretex and slickers.
So easy to absorb the dry warmth
the harmless music, the coffee scent,
the flatness of the gray outside.

A black umbrella glides by the window
a yellow fleece shirt plops in a chair.
Green baristas slide left and right
cash register to espresso machine.
In an unconsciously unified effort,
ease of movement, ease of day
politely synchronize the gray.

The traffic light, the only color
outside, the only spring foliage,
turns from green to yellow
as traffic at the four corners stops;
on cue the tulips close up and leave
just as cold, wet and naïve.

3/25/04

After his second job he rolled home

in the 15-year-old pickup
with the iffy radiator and the bald retreads,
stopped at the traffic light: Red.
He yawned, rubbed his eyes: Red.
Five sixteen-hour days drains the soul,
he yawns, but smiles, tapping the plastic
enclosed picture of a six-year-old girl,
shivering gently under the truck's laborious drone.
"Another eight months, little girl.
Another eight months."
The green light admits passage
from the bowels of the industrial area
through the haphazard transition to Suburbia
with green lawns and magnolias and azaleas.
He ignores the snapshot Utopia
and slows for another traffic light,
glancing at the 4X6 taped to the dashboard:
An eight-year-old boy in a soccer uniform.
"Just give me eight months, little guy.
Eight months to kiss it goodbye."
Green. He passes a clean-looking
cookie-cutter apartment complex,
never imagining it as an aspiration, a hope.
He stares at the building as it transfers to the jiggling rear-view mirror,
and the truck arrives at the outskirts
of a little town, in the gravel parking lot
of a converted building, square, gray.
The caretaker signs him into the shelter
and he drags himself and his
warehouse-scented sweatshirt up the stairs
and before that ascent a bright little face
blocks his path and jumps into his
unexpecting arms, beaming.
Fatigue bypasses irritation, forms a smile,
cracking the stubbly stare, and he
holds the little girl close, tight.

She ignores his smell, his stubble.
She smiles and kisses and hugs.
She talks into his neck.
"Did the big software company call today, Daddy?"
"Not today, punkin."
They ascend quietly.
"We'll be OK, Daddy. I found a lucky penny."
"Yeah?"
"Uh huh. It said: Eight months to a new house."
"Sounds good to me, sweetie."
"What does trickle down mean, Daddy?"
"No idea, sweetie. No idea."

3/26/04

For reasons yet unclear

we swarmed their country
deposed their dictator
and deposed their culture
looking for weapons not found
looking for terrorists not found
looking for a silver lining
finding a country in tatters
finding petrified children
finding slow grinding death.

For reasons yet unclear
four people trying to help, died -
shot, maimed, dismembered, burned.
Dragged behind a truck around Falluja.
Too gruesome to show.
Too gruesome to tell.
Too gruesome to know.
Any more detail.
Any more truth .
Any more spin.

For reasons yet unclear
mothers watch their sons
pack their bags and head to the base
following orders of a madman
following orders spawned from hubris
following orders under freedom's veil
into the path of darkness
into the path of death
into the path of history's harsh glare.

4/5/04

We continue to measure

our Democracy
in platitudes and body bags
heedless of the Vietnam lesson
heedless of the decimated families
and History's shaking finger.

We continue to console ourselves,
with the words fed to us on plastic platters
and water cooler wisdom:
"Freedom isn't free."
"They hate our freedom."

We continue to watch passively
as we acquiesce to invasions
at home and abroad
as our very language devolves
soundbite by soundbite.

We repeat the mantras
of our democratically appointed regime
"A uniter, not a divider."
"Democracy for all."
"You're with us or against us."

We repeat the mantras
of our entertaining patron saints
swallowing whole the Christly Passions
swallowing whole all the reasons
for invading, killing and stealing.

We repeat the mistakes of our past
and resolute, proudly, in red white blue
chant them again today.

4/9/04

They roll in threes

So floats the myth
Laid out by an observant sage
Many moons and beaches ago
Sunset long past
White foamy ridges in the
Murky night water
Surf a constant roar
Soothing peaceful paradoxical
Waves crush rocks into sand
Over eons
Playing children
Mooning new couples
Skinnydipping teens
All create the life of this sandalwood
The cliffs preside
They persist like the wind,
They watch without judgment;
Only time,
Only humans
Practice that harsh craft.

The life of the sand
We all contribute
Like dinosaurs and chiton
Before us
The sand
Outlasts us all.

4/16/04

The Puget Sound rains

stopped just long enough
to let the colors explode-
magnolia, dogwood, cherry, azalea
simple colors, delicious smells
of another verdant Northwest spring.

The restlessness rains,
pours in our shoe box cotton ball country
little kids trying to see out the window
jumping, bouncing, catching glimpses
of horror, or shaking fists,
burning American flags, coffins.

Penetrating questions rain
on the adults near the window.
"Help me see out there," we plead.
"Later, maybe. Kool-Aid?"
We step away from the window, uneasy.
We stop bouncing, stop looking.

The Puget Sound rains
darken the sky again
the storm rushes the valley
leaves, branches, flowers scatter everywhere,
reason scatters everywhere
propaganda pollen on my windshield.

Hold me up to the window.
Help me see what I already know.

5/2/04

Lean on the bar

Lean on the podium
I want to smack that smirk
Right off your simian face.

On your own, though,
On your own without
Karl or Karen pulling strings
Or scripting or miming – oh boy.

Hand in the cookie jar
Deer in the headlights
Long, griping pauses
Pathetic self-effacing humor.

Lean on the podium
Lean on the smarmy coterie
Of sycophants and spectators
Assuring the righteous.

Your minions feather your bed
Your minions obscure your past
We thought we voted otherwise
But you stuck around anyway.

Life catches up, though:
Life catches up, even though it's slow,
When you dig your hole with a shovel
And you fill it up with a spoon.

5/6/04

What passes for steadfast resolve

in your circle of sycophants
barely rates stubborn ignorance
and blinding incompetence in mine.

What passes for patriotism
among your devoted serfs
looks like Constitutional crime
down here among mortals.

The carefully scripted photo op.
The Lincoln Landing.
The Rushmore Freezeframe.
The Plastic Turkey.
The Firefight Hug.

Play "dress-up" on your own time.
Let a real person be President
Costume parties promise fun;
Dressing up like a President doesn't make you one.

5/19/04

The cycling shorts sweatsuit

casual baggypants crowd
avoid the netherworld of midweek,
locked in their quiet gray mazes,
Labyrinthine Steelcase corridors
of feigned importance and gravitas.

Just the retirees, the unemployed and me,
in our little silos, communally
sipping coffee and tea,
oblivious to the death of midweek,
obvious dearth of commerce and urgency,
schoolkids on field trips, little noses
pressed against cafe' glass, smearing
nose and pawprints and questions
in the midmorning sun,
traffic lazily rolling through the laissez-faire intersection,
occasional blossom falling from
the ornamental cherry in
the bank parking lot.

Employees gossip behind the counter,
no business like somebody else's
muzak tinkles clearly, unimpeded
by customer chatter.
The gray maze people, five days
away from their Saturday morning incursion,
continue with posturing and memos,
silently wishing for life during the week.

6/8/04

Shorts and sun dresses

Casual Friday all summer long
Steamed milk yields to ice in lattes
And another cool cloudy Independence Day
on tap with beer and legal explosives.

They relax outside the cafe'
under the green canvas umbrella,
drinks on the table
lazy dog under,
relaxed repose in the plastic chairs
noon breeze pushing the skinny maples
east and west, rustling napkins
and crumbs on the glass table.

Three men – Asian, Thai, Balinese -
hell, I guess badly. I wonder
at their ease, how easy they appear,
at ease their demeanor conducts
itself in chuckles, smiles, stillness.
Clearly foreigners, obviously American.
What meaning the night
need hold for them remains enigmatic
for me, awash in the turmoil
of current events and politics;

At the end of the day the year the life
the purpose must sparkle like the
finale over Elliot Bay:
Easier to love, my brothers.
Much easier to love.

7/3/04

Small perfect letters

Slanting across the
Small perfect page in his
Small perfect life
Diving out of harm's way
Avoiding passion like stormy weather
He picks up the ancient pen
and opens the leather bound journal
spreads it across the heavy maple desk
in the small perfect room
where those small perfect thoughts
fill volumes and tomes
as life flies by outside his window
past his suspiciously clean coffee mug
and drill-sergeant-taut desktop
past the decades in flux and wonder
and the women and drama
The reflection in the night window
only tells the truth
Incapable of living
in a small perfect pane
bordered by the limits
of space and time
Exposing all those frailties
and riskless nights since
in a small imperfect litany
of silent, well-intentioned
glances into a haphazard mirror,
squinting first, then looking into
the darkness beyond.

8/19/04

Sunday religiousity pitched virtuosity

Trickle down sermons
And third-party counseling -
No real coffee at that table
Old guys to the left,
a litany of valves
and cars and cost
Bereft of sun and the
late church crowd,
this remains at large,
weak eavesdrop fodder
Leaving me crippled and forced to rely weakly
on my own feeble mind,
no grist for the spoof mill,
nobody really tipping
the caricature needle into the red
The nicely dressed religious
righteous chatter continues
with no signs of scanning
the congregation for snoring,
some poor bastard trying
in vain to read a book
next to the gaudy magpies
while the gravelly-voiced
car buffs have switched
to droning on about fish
Accepting the fate of
this literary hangover,
I put my pen down
and sip coffee, eat cookie.

8/22/04

11/14/04 Bucky's 4th & Meeker

The Simian King,
his fossilized gang of ruthless sycophants:
Red State, White State
No more Blue State
I got me a mandate
An Ohio Florida license to hate
Reach across the aisle
and screw you with a smile
I promise to work with you,
Just think the way I do:
Outlaw critical thinking,
Favor heavy drinking
Virtuous vitriol, brain share shrinking
But the economy keeps sinking
You smirk, unblinking:
Ain't gonna change a thing.
"Give me your tired, your poor —
and we'll make those lazy
bastards our slaves, too."
Proud to be Red White, No Blue.
Different thoughts? Fuck you.
Not enough money? Fuck you, too.
Just enough work to stay poor
keep the shine on the mall floor
accidental right wrong values whore
We must work together, compromise
(With your greasy burger, you want fries?)
You elitist bastards lost, now apologize.
Well hold on, Curious George, not so fast
I got your mandate; this too shall pass.
Mandate? Mandate, my ass.

161

We return to the haze

We emerge from relaxation
We slink back to what passes
for reality
for importance
We punish ourselves
We deny ourselves
We refuse the right
of happiness
of completion
We leave the sun,
We retreat from the sand,
We say behaving slowly
contradicts reality
fosters laziness
We insist sadness works,
We mandate sobriety
We create virtue
from pain
from commerce
We cross our eyes
We grimace and grunt,
We wonder aloud
why we live far away from here
why life lives differently there.
We pack the games and souvenirs
We circle the rooms again,
We lock the door one last time
Drop the key at the office,
Drop the happiness at the beach,
And hope
We trapped a memory
for the ages.

11/22/04

The more I wander along the shore

startling muskrats and frogs
Rambunctious mental wingbeats
not really achieving liftoff or flight
maintaining stability on the thin branch
the waxwing clinging to the black locust
I look for metaphors.
Stupidest goddamn pastime on earth.
I wonder aloud at my world
and I write it down in here.
With no sense of decency or profanity
I ignore the migraines until
the page blurs, I break my own rules
and the words look like the transcript
of a bar fight in downtown somewhere.
Too young for senility too old for stupidity
too confused to choose.
Great. I killed another snail.
Trying to concentrate out here proves useless.
I pull weeds and drop them right away,
managing to keep clarity at bay
just a little while longer.
Lawn looks big enough for whiffle ball or golf.
How much longer?
The spinning continues
despite my whiny protests
and the ducks and geese yell at each other
and at least I understand, now,
why the frogs and muskrats hide.

9/7/05

I turned to the sun a final time

A wild guess for the unwilling, unaware
Satori eluded me up until now, fishing
No bait, just standing there on the dock
Squinting into that flaming orange ball
I never saw it as red, only acquiesced,
A final look maybe before dying, silence
Or maybe before the serious drinking starts.
Nothing matters, at this point.
I laugh, wishing I knew the specifics
I hate the poets, the experience – starved
academics who judge the laity inferior
failing to disguise their own emotion.
I hate my own judgmental sarcasm.
Meandering up the lawn accidentally
pissed off not noticing the loss of summer
or how light the oars on my shoulder
I always saw the sky's curve, too,
and I acquiesce again, nailing the right answer
pleased grins from everyone, failing myself.
The big orange hell ball crushes itself
on the firs at the end of the lake.
The oars rattle in the shed as the door shuts.
The streaked pink sky and the lake
swallow the pitiful satori and the bullfrogs
take over with meaningless braying,
Nothing remains, nothing sure.

9/17/05

The sluggishness of a fall day returns

The pen feels like a bowling ball on a needle
with a throw rug wrapped around the nib
Emerging from a pundit-induced stupor
I stagger about the house like an old drunk
So many voices caw for attention
So many bright lights fight for eyeshare.
And this defines us: Loud flashy idiots.
I ceded the battle for lucid thought today.
I shuffle through the kitchen
foraging for processed foodstuffs,
Navy blue sweatpants dragging the floor
for crumbs and lint, the only details
missing from the image, an offramp
or a refrigerator box, the migraine leaving me
useless, scattered, mumbling about bleu cheese
and hormone-laced two percent milk
and what a dolt the President is. As if
a coherent though might pop up behind
the leftover spaghetti and week-old tuna
I know better.
Too much talk radio reality TV weapons
of mass media no time to think just act eat buy.
We look at the sky in wonder not awe
When we look we fail to understand
what we see fail to question what we know.
And I stare at the old cheese
under the able guidance of a 40-watt bulb
and that cheese, mold and all,
makes as much sense as anything.

9/18/05

A fluid catastrophe of events unfold daily

bombards me with news of a desperately stupid man,
running a country into the ground
as horrified spectators witness epic idiocy,
millions duped, robbed, and slaughtered by the hour.
Knowing too much.
Thinking too much.
Feeling too much.
Long ago last year five years
personal hell caused pain
divorce, cancer, adultery, feuds, hair color -
but today: An act of Congress. Presidential decree.
And the obligatory half-hour spot on Fox News.
I squint at the sun stabbing through the blinds
and turn off all the noise. How to proceed?
My living wage job? My frivolous pursuits?
Failure! Constant, unrelenting failure.
Soon the energy star fluorescent bulbs take over.
With the creamy hypnotic artificial light
spilling into my pores I begin to understand
why they all go nuts, eventually, all those writers.
All that thinking!
All that feeling!
No more knowing!
Pissing into a tidal wave
not even able to register the sliver of warmth
before giving in to the sea.

9/19/05

Rain and engines

Howling hissing wind
Talk radio cacophony
Never mind the mindless chatter
Bouncing off the bony pate
My head, my holograph
Truck smells like socks
Tucked in an armpit
And the gray day
Whooshes by, unhindered
by my presence, my insistence
of being driving breathing
A hundred miles of I-5
So many stories between mileposts
Kids, wives, spilled Sprite
and rest area hot chocolate
loud music, snoring passengers -
So much life lived in the cab
of the smelly black truck,
waiting for chapters to begin
transitions to end,
all the driving to stop.

11/2/05

The birch rotted from the inside,

oblivious, blown to the ground at Christmas
Caused a geyser in the yard
Pulp burned in the fire pit. Marshmallows
a serenade of frogs and crickets,
meeting at the water's edge, ducks
and otters hiding in the reeds
gentle slapping at the bulkhead
so many sounds such noisy silence
And the effort to see
The effort to be
So much converging as the birch hit the ground
Red Christmas sweater
Guests on the way, hot buttered rum
Too much comfort, fresh air
I see the bubbling ground in my slippers
And find the master shutoff.
So much to postpone
Repaired in spring warmth, oh but
the tree's self-amputation resides
in my head, in the spigot now lifeless
The contradictory astuteness of rural fact.
Broke. Fix it. No.
Renegade winds ride again
Fast and violent quiet and sure
I love the hate I fear here
So sure, so quiet.

12/24/05

The American flag flaps wildly

Against the deep gray spring sky
Against all reason and logic.

Celebrate the Dutch heritage
the cheery blonde, blue-eyed history
Perseverance and grace.

Raspberries, dairies and beef
Acres and acres of silage and manure
Open sky fresh air clean living.

New Holland, Husqvarna, Kubota
Modern methods mean more money
Greater yield, greater profits for Agribiz.

They live in trailers next to the fields
Corn and berries surround their summer home
Low pay, long season, no questions.

They run the berry pickers
Hernandez, I think. And sons.
They stop at dusk. In September.

They heft potatoes into huge trucks
Rodriquez, I think.
They stop at dusk. In October.

The "Dutch" kids move to cities.
Easy work, better pay.
American flags only today.

5/6/06

Sluggish late spring

early summer lilac
permeates penetrates
explosion of colors
sirens sounds bounce
off the sallow lake
through the open windows
intoxicated sweet smells
Languorous sensuous ideal
textbook colors scenes
pastoral idyllic van Gogh
how appropriate here in
this Rockwell fake Dutch town
No manure smells tonight
no John Deere feere on the roads
Just dogwood and lilac in the dark
let it touch you in the night
you hear everything tonight
the lake the geese the cars
even the stars seem loud tonight
so quiet pure serene night sky
paradoxical slow rapid silent harmonies
a lover's breath, caresses
a soothing cacophony of noiseless motion
still and vital,
so loud brilliant black and quiet
a petal in my palm all around me
Surround confront the point engulf
This night

5/16/06

170

A slate of haze hangs over the valley.
My head throbs with the day's weight
Coffeeshop conversations freckle the ambience
Or whatever.
Morning in America
Summer in the Promised Land.
All promises.
They trickle in, not knowing
of the Dow crumbling,
of the four new dead Marines today
of the rapid loss of species
of Kilimanjaro without snow
Of Divine Strake
of a nuclear-powered redux.
Such travesties of promise

Accidental breeze stirs the trees
My eyes abrade the uds or vice versa
Iraq Darfur, Afghanistan
Three of many we fail to understand
We soothe ourselves here
Coffee and inanity
dribble onto the table
absorbed with napkins
and sitcoms and cars and happy.

All accumulations
All collections
All vibrant reminders
of our place on the great big ball

I no longer know who rules

Who pries my eyelids open at 5:30 a.m.
Who insists I drive to work in my stupor
I see them all puttering about their day
Calm and official and important
Hiding who knows what under the biz duds,
Under the placid professional exteriors
Maybe they rule.
Maybe they understand,
Because after I put my hours in
After I take one for the team,
After I endure my commute
I stand alone in my house wondering
How I ended up here
With this particular consciousness
With this particular set of agonies
The pointless job and the meaningless skills
The relentless posturing and posing
The continuous pleasing of strangers -
If it disappeared tomorrow
If it vanished in a heartbeat
If it dissolved like a "have a nice day,"
I would miss it like the last square
Like the tattered remnants,
Like the last bit of toilet paper
Stuck to the cardboard roll.
I no longer know who rules
But I bet, when I find out,
The old man
Spits fire, raw fire.

5/30/06

172

Permutations of sameness

Gray Christmas carols
Aimless shiftless scheppy
Caffeine patrons addicts
Oh I dare not judge
I sit in no throne
I guard my latte
with bloodshot eyes and four days
of vacation stubble as you do
We lull ourselves
Into the strip mall coffeeshop oasis
With stripmallcoffeshop jazzcarols
And so much pleasantry
And so much niceness
We keep coming back
We keep getting high
On nubile vibrating baristas
and absurdly expensive coffee fixes
So pleasant so sincere
The Hooters of Arabica Beans
We relish these few days
Before we drag ourselves
Back toward the spinning blades
of Corporate America, wool barely
covering fang these days,
Wondering wordlessly in little
islands of doubt, how to end
the spiral without suicide, how
to find Christmas, and stay there.

12/19/06

No more dead poets,
angling for publication,

gave up long ago their ostentatious
attempts at reconciliation:
Speaking to other dead poets
from beyond the grave of academia,
and only the sound and stench of corpses with pens remain
They stopped writing for you long ago.
Like exquisite Swiss chocolate:
Too good for kids and Blue Collar.
And White Collar eats Snickers.
Reads "People."
Such rarefied air we share
We Elitist Pricks
With our meters and iambs and trochees,
picky vegans at Mel's Diner
Dilettantes in Professional Life,
Hobbyists of no tangible skill
Never quite admitting our envy
Never quite participating
Never digging the splinter
from the heel of the hand
with a sewing needle
Never sleeping over the propellers
of a fishing boat in the Bering Sea.

Yet the lofty language of learning
permeates volumes accessible only
to those deemed worthy of the stories
and never those who live.

10/31/07

174

Six billion of us on this crowded ball

The final approach to Armageddon,
The curtain call of humans and bees
Nope, not global warming
Nope, not a nuclear holocaust
Nope, not worldwide poverty
Follow the commuter
Follow the police
Follow the trucker
The work evades
Purpose eludes us all
Meaning evaporated faster
Than our balding ozone layer
And cynicism beat out the locusts
We entertained ourselves stupid:
TV kills
We consumed and crapped and mated
Faster that gypsy moths
We invaded habitats like English Ivy
And happily strangled our hosts
We drove ourselves insane with cool drugs
And beached ourselves with Capitalism
While whales got lost at sea.

So when the warm tsunami
Wipes out Omaha and we
Sip our pina coladas under
A palm tree in Nome, take heart:
Eight planets left.

11/10/07

Essays and Short Stories

Flying Home

The airport in Manchester, New Hampshire is convenient and quiet compared to SeaTac in Seattle. It had been eleven years since I had had a chance to compare the two, having bolted to the Northwest 17 years earlier, leaving all family behind. Desperation borne of ignorance, curiosity and dysfunction, a stultifying town, and the hubris of a 19-year-old with a life to live and something to prove.

I don't know, really. All those cliches work, to some extent, but why does anybody make a grand exit like that, anyway?
I just *had* to.

Home. It's supposed to conjure up images of serenity, of warm nights and cordial words, of everyone at the table, sharing a meal, playing a game. Christmas in pajamas, barely awake parents, bounding kids, spicy smells and snow outside.

It can bring up the opposite, too. Ghettos or gated communities, rife with money's stench, of what it can and can't do to people, the barrenness of having too much or nothing, the depravity of addiction or nonchalance.

Another loaded word: Family. Togetherness. Comfort. Support. Where you return when the world is too harsh and real. Awfully hard to separate it from "home," really.

I was flying "home" to see my "family."

It was early October, 8:30 p.m., Eastern Time, though my watch still thought it was in Seattle. Six hours in the air. The wife I married a year ago was holding my hand as we headed toward Baggage Claim, wondering aloud why the airport seemed to be so quiet.

"It's just a regional airport," I said, somewhat apologetically.

"Yeah, but everything's closed," she said, swinging her head toward a dark newsstand and a few gated gift shops. "It's 8:30 on a Saturday night!"

"Welcome to New Hampshire."

The next day we set out to visit my mother in my hometown, and maybe take a spin through the neighborhood where I grew up, so my wife could have some sort of historical context for me, the way I did with her in West Seattle. She had heard about the violence, alcoholism, emotional abuse, denial, and slow healing. Now she would meet the players and see the set.

Here's what I expected: A tiny white house with black trim, the European larch permitting a gauzy view of the little wedge of land between an old barn and a dilapidated duplex on a little stretch of uneven pavement called Walcott Ave.

I expected May and the lilac intoxication for those first few weeks of warm when the big bushes displayed their color and vigor. I expected August and the cacophony of odor from the barn next door: Pig and cow dung, plus the occasional aroma of swill being slow-cooked in a big brick cauldron, stirred patiently by the barn's owner, Phil, with an old garden spade. I expected the big catalpa to the left of the tiny house to be dropping its long beans every now and then, and the striated white blossoms to vie for attention amid the lilac's insistence, and the big leaves to shade me from oppressive humidity. I expected October's bite in the air in the morning, and the freakish heat by midday, and brilliant color all the time, everywhere. I expected February and snow covering the top landing of the three concrete steps up to the shabby little door, and the subzero cold that follows, biting through to the bone past whatever high-tech fiber I tossed in front of it.

I expected nothing to change there, and I expected to feel nothing like I did then, growing up in a place of intense narrow-mindedness and blinkard cynicism and a blind contempt for curiosity and possibility. I expected my painstakingly acquired open-mindedness and objectivity to put all conflict aside and embrace this pitiful little place as my original home, and forgive it its past sins and foibles.

Now I was driving a rented minivan on this early October day, with my Seattle-born wife in the passenger seat, the voice of objectivity—somebody who had never traveled east of the Mississippi—eagerly recalling aloud to her all the stuff that had changed or stayed the same. "That used to be Mickey's garage, there used to be a traffic circle here, there was a barber shop right there, I used to get groceries there, that used to be Archie's place, oh wow—that bakery's still

179

in business, jeez, the post office moved?" It must have looked strange to her, this catalog of enthusiastic historical edits. I mean, I actually sounded excited about seeing the place again, and apart from my immediate family and two close friends, had never said anything positive to my wife about it.

I grew up here, then I grew up 3400 miles away, in a place nothing like it. In the years since my father's death, I kept checking in on "My Perspective" like my mother used to check her roast beef. I did this with the question: "Could I live there again?" My reaction, even in the most dire times, was typically a quick, "Hell, no." I would get the dysfunctional alcoholic family flashbacks, the searing lack of confidence, the artificial poverty, the head games, the mistrust, and the blinding conflict of loving and hating one's parents. Constantly. It took years to get to the point where it was all consuming and unbearable, and I had to assume it would take years for that feeling to dissipate. So I'd open that emotional oven door once in awhile to see where I was, how my psyche was healing.

We soon arrived at the cross street that led to the house where I grew up. The expectations started to fall like those colorful leaves in the first bracing windstorm of the year. Everything was smaller in scale. Houses had been added to vacant lots. Existing houses were much closer together than I remember. It seemed immediately preposterous that Phil used to stick his cows in these fields to graze on summer days. As I wondered how Phil had been spending his time these days, we rolled slowly in front of my childhood home.

What I saw next was a travesty of aesthetics rivaling Las Vegas. Instead of the tiny white house with black trim, my view was that of a garish green shoebox with a blunt snout tenuously tacked to its side, with inexplicable lattice towers sprouting out of its . . . well . . . hind end. And of course, what would a house of this caliber be without those tasteful, historically accurate, retina-burning green shutters with Lucky Charms shapes cut out of their middles? What could I do but put the minivan in "Park", grab the camera and start shooting? I didn't see the catalpa, but I did remember my mother telling me it had been damaged in the wake of a September hurricane a few years ago, and had to be taken down. The barn looked empty, and it also looked like it was about

to mate with the green alien. The larch, now twice the size of what I remember, seemed to be doing its best to hide the whole thing, but I don't think three or four redwoods could have blocked the radioactive greenness beaming defiantly from that little gem.
I clicked the shutter and advanced the film slowly, as if I were witnessing the first real human-alien encounter. In a sense, I was. This suddenly wasn't the house I grew up in—this was now paranormal. The original was never something to be called "beautiful" but it had an honesty about it the casual observer could at least respect. But this—this looked like it belonged on the set of "The X-Files."

When I put the camera down, I said something profound, like, "Holy mackerel," and my wife, wide-eyed, shook her head slowly and said, "Wow. I'm sorry, honey."

So small. So crowded. So . . . what? We lingered there in front of the short driveway as I tried to get a grip on my dismay. Really, why did it bother me? It wasn't as if it were sacred ground; my childhood certainly had its warm moments, but was far from idyllic. I didn't particularly miss anyone there, apart from my immediate family.

It was a predictably bad moment to check the oven, but I did. "Hell, no" screeched the roast beef, and the little van pulled away with two bewildered Seattleites.

The feeling persisted even as we visited with my mother and her new husband in their little apartment not two miles away from the alien encampment. Mom brought out the old photo album and we all smiled and winced at the various candids of different stages of our lives. My wife got a kick out of the grinning kid with the big head and crewcut, standing on the lawn with the barn in the background. It looked so open, not like the claustrophobic little compound I saw a half-hour earlier. I was the pumpkin on the stick, of course. The photo took me right into the tone of the scene; objectively, it was not a great place to live, but it wasn't the worst, either. I never went hungry; I never looked dirty, unkempt, or neglected. I was an excellent student. And not too many years after that photo was taken, all I ever wanted to do was to get out of there. So why this nagging need for sentiment, 30 years later?

"Accidental." The word slipped into my consciousness when my wife began to react verbally to her surroundings. "It looks like this just sprouted up off the freeway." I mentally forgave her the confusion of "freeway" for "turnpike", and noted that although she didn't use the word "accidental," it was clearly implied. And she was right. Nothing about the town was conscious or deliberate. The place is a big basal brainstem function; other cities were cerebral. My hometown was little more than a twitch or a tic in the course of a long day. Other cities and towns conversed; this one grunted.

Accidental. It was true. Most of the roads in New England, in fact, weren't planned, but simply sprung up out of well-worn horse trails in the days of pilgrims, witches and tea parties. My hometown was no different that way. Other places, though, seemed to cope with it differently. The towns surrounding my hometown weren't exactly New England hotspots, but they did carry a different sort of attitude or character, in that they actually *had* character. Although my hometown had been around since the early 1700s, it had all the character of a zit-faced teenager watching MTV. No major industry to speak of, no cultural amenities that it cared to tout (yet the Franco-American heritage is remarkable there)--nothing. Just more typical American strip mall mentality: Make it all the same. So along the main road going through town there were lots of medical facilities for old folks, too-large supermarkets, convenience stores, gas stations, KFC, Pizza Hut, Taco Bell, and the ubiquitous Dunkin' Donuts. All like nondescript mushrooms clinging to the base of trees in the woods.

After my wife and I left my mom's apartment, we headed toward my sister's house, roughly 40 minutes to the south. There were some lulls in our chatter as we played back the events of the day, and in those lulls both of us would look out at the rolling landscape speckled with red and gold, each seeing differently, interpreting this rich tapestry of time. My wife was seeing it from historical and geographical windows, comparing it to Seattle's youth and planned roads and freeways; I saw it from a sense of place. I noticed the little town line markers defining each boundary we passed. Dover. Madbury. Durham. Lee. Epping. Gradually I realized I was doing that with this sense of place of mine: Old man. Confused kid. Sage. Idiot. Patience.

And here's what I didn't expect: It was worse than I remembered. All the stuff I railed at as a kid, as a hormone-driven teenager, and as a young adult were right on the mark, and then some. The place is *awful.* I deliberately did not say anything that might slant my wife's experience of the place, but as soon as we were on the road to my sister's house, she breathed, "Wow, that place is really a pit." I felt a bit of redemption then, and yet . . .I had to check the oven again. Things were clearing up, as if I had to have a set of objective eyes to assure me that I wasn't a hostile witness in this case of nostalgic identity. I didn't get a "Hell no," this time, but I did get, "Well, hell no, not *there.*" I relaxed. "Home" had always been such an important word to me, and it hurt to reduce it to four letters. Home wasn't that caricature of the dwelling I grew up in, home wasn't in the horrid school system of small-minded sycophants, home wasn't a Dunkin' Donuts every twenty yards or the high school or the Wal-Mart.

Home was a mom that outlived World War II, the Korean War, and alcoholism. Home was a sister whose sense of self and character guided her to a warm, wonderful family in rural New Hampshire. Home was a wife, in a rented minivan with Massachusetts plates, who thought New Hampshire was pretty cool, even if my hometown was a pit. Home was Portsmouth, Kingston, Rye, North Conway, Bartlett, Danville, Antrim, Wolfeboro - all of these and none of these.

Home is reveling in every season, every smell, every sight and sound, and every human I choose to place in my life. Home is people I trust with my life, my love, every day, everywhere.

Too soon, we found ourselves back in the little airport, our bags full of maple syrup, red leaves between paperback pages, photos, sweatshirts, and a real fondness for funky accents. We didn't talk much. Part of that was exhaustion, to be sure, but part of that was sadness, too. For my wife, I can guess that it must have been establishing a connection with my immediate family very quickly and taking a liking to all of them, then departing just as quickly. For me, though, it was knowing that I *missed* my home.

*First Place Short Story winner, Write on the Beach Contest 2003

Persistent Ruthlessness

By 1990, my life had been disintegrating for quite awhile, and here was its synthesis: I was with my soon-to-be-ex-lover in the Harvard Exit Theater in Seattle's Capitol Hill, watching the film adaptation of Andre Brink's novel, "A Dry White Season." The images of torture, the messages of apartheid racism, and the consciousness that my own pathetic miseries paled so deeply in comparison to what was happening all around me left me a crying, hysterical mess in the theater by the film's closing minutes, and through the lobby, into the light of a dying summer's afternoon. I couldn't look at her, and I couldn't look at myself the same way anymore. The film was over, we were over, but the aftertaste was still strong and bitter, and the question that seared me to the quick then still does today: How can one human being do that to another?

I would wrestle with the question repeatedly in literature ("1984"), current events (El Salvador, and Guatemalan covert wars), and even more films. I couldn't get rid of it years later, when, with my first wife, I saw "Boyz in the Hood" and found myself sobbing, though not quite as poignantly as the first instance. The question persisted. How on earth...?

For my own sanity, I gave myself a crash course in South African history, beginning shortly before the Boer War, and up through the (then) current day. Though I found a temporal logic to the events, I never found an answer there, either. And there would be sufficient anecdotal support that the act of deliberately maiming other people has been around as long as the psyche itself, so I had somehow better get used to it and take a more pragmatic, realistic approach, and to stop being such a goddamned idealist wimp.

I suppose, for most, it's one of those questions like, "Is there really alien life out there?" Some would argue the odds of the universe and say, "Of course there is," and others would argue the empirical facts: "We have no evidence there is." The question then, persists; there remains a possibility. As does the fundamental question, are humans basically good or essentially evil? A great philosophical conundrum, that, but little more. Questions like these allow us to spin our wheels a bit and perhaps get a little mental exercise, but they don't really help us think or behave differently; certainly we don't.

For a while, I could live within myself, knowing that the specter of malignant behavior was very far away, and while disturbing, seemed to be contained. But today the queasy helplessness returns in the form of photo CDs from Abu Ghraib, and Internet videos of people being beheaded simply for being associated with the wrong group. Isn't war ruthless enough? Isn't the psychological damage of seeing your house and family reduced to a pile of wreckage and pink dust permanent enough? Apparently not. Now we humans hunt each other in very specific, very intentional, and very sadistic ways to force each other to see a particular point of view. You will tell us who bombed us or we will electrocute you slowly, via your genitalia. We will pierce your eardrums with burning cigarettes. We will stalk you like deer. We will shoot you, we will blow you to a million pieces while you sleep. We will explode you and your car as soon as you open that door. We will chain you to a post and let hungry dogs chew on your ankles. You will sleep in your own urine and feces until you tell us what we want to hear. We will assassinate every one of you using any means necessary. But no matter what, we will be heard.

Surely then, my answers must be getting closer. "How can one human being do that to another?" My ideology is superior to yours. My god is bigger than yours. Sometimes, one must be cruel to be kind. Sometimes, the village must be destroyed to be saved. This information is so vital, we will stop at nothing to get it.

This naïveté was exacerbated by personal strife: Ending a long relationship, lousy job, no money. And of course, impotence in the teeth of current events. I understood nothing of how the politics of civil rights works. I just knew that for some visceral reason, I couldn't stand to see people torture each other, even if they were actors.

My life got better. I ended up marrying a wonderful woman who likes green apples and fondue. She doesn't care about my spreading bald spot or midsection. She lets me be me. We're not wealthy, but we're not starving. Our kids behave and misbehave. Our dog snores. We live an absurdly typical American life. I write and write and write.

And when forced to confront the persistent ruthlessness of warlike minds, I speak out against them when I can. I protest, I rally. I yell at my congressman and I shriek in the local paper. There must still be some hope that triumphs over the cynicism in my life, because I still go through the motions as if I might be heard.

But as I watch my son play soccer on a foggy wet field, as I see my daughter play her clarinet on a grand old stage, as I note the 60th anniversary of the closing of Auschwitz through the lens of today's media, and as I flip through the Rolodex of our brief history on this planet, even the recent past: Soweto, Bosnia, Darfur, Abu Ghraib—as I watch my kids try to make sense of sports and music and fun and work and learning, I can easily see the day when we're in the car, headed home, and they'll put down the GameBoys in the back seat and let a few miles pass before they consider what they accidentally heard that day or that week. They'll watch I-5 disappear through the Skagit Valley as it snakes through Arlington. They'll take me by surprise, and even though I know it's unavoidable and I've rehearsed the answer a thousand times, I won't be ready. "Why did people do that stuff in those prisons, Daddy?"

I can see my head shaking, my shoulders shrugging, and I can hear my voice doing exactly what drives me nuts when my 10-year old son does it: "I don't know." Fifteen years and two lifetimes later, I still don't know how people can achieve the depraved equilibrium that allows an Auschwitz, a Soweto, a Bosnia, an Abu Ghraib.

I will drive on, and the question will linger in the back seat for a few more miles, and I will once again hear the silly bubbly tunes of the GameBoy as the Everett skyline comes into view on our way toward Seattle. I will be reminded again of the Harvard Exit and my sobbing sprint to my car and an escape from a life I couldn't understand, and I will hope my ignorance keeps me human.

Fat Molly

I barge into my apartment's solitude, leaving a trail of clothes behind as I head straight for a hot shower. Another day of placating executives, and all I want is: No thinking. Passing through the bedroom for a fresh change of clothes, I glance out the window and an object catches my eye. I'm on the third floor and there's a big pine tree that's a little taller than the building and about fifteen feet away, so this thing is pretty much at eye level. I move cautiously toward the window because I'm still naked and I don't want to be known in the complex as "the weird naked guy in Building H," so I sidestep a bit and get closer. It's a cat. A big brown tabby with a tiny head. Hmmm, not just big, a FAT brown tabby. Dog must've treed her.

Well, it's a good thing I sneak up on the window because there's a woman down there, frantically calling for the cat in what can only be described as a caterwaul, partly pitiable and mostly irritating. "Please come down, Molly, puh-leeeeeeeeeeeeeeze come dooowwwwn." Pretty soon it's like a slow-motion car alarm that won't stop, and now it's attracting a crowd.

First they come out because they want this poor little psycho to shut the hell up, then she points to the tree (almost at me, but nobody notices: all eyes are on the obese feline swaying gently in the afternoon breeze), and they understand.

Next, the corniest thing happens: Somebody has apparently called the fire department, because here comes one of those mammoth red trucks, bouncing crazily over the myriad speed mines in the main drive of the complex. This is nuts, of course. It's an apartment complex; there's a maintenance crew here. They surely have an extension ladder somewhere. Somebody is obviously from Mayberry RFD or very old. On further reflection, though, the maintenance crew would probably still be filling out work orders and signing liability releases as the cat lost weight and starved to death up there in the breeze, so maybe the fire department idea's not so dumb.

The crowd, I'm guessing, is The Dumpster People. No, they don't live in dumpsters or rescue old pizza from them. It's just that the dumpsters are infrequently emptied in the complex, and people wait for the garbage truck to bounce its way through so they can run out to the dumpsters as fast as they can while there's still room for bountiful trash. Kind of amusing, really: They watch through parted blinds and doors ajar, and as soon as the driver's in the truck headed for the exit, Whoosh! Out they come like ants to sugar. So it's your standard mob mentality out there, just the mouth-breathing, knuckledragging throng with a blank-faced interest in somebody else's anguish.

Like a cell dividing, the crowd parts to let someone through. It's the wiry old crone from Building C. Annie, Fanny, something like that. She's prying the crowd apart with her hickory cane, making her way toward the fire truck. "What in God's name took you so long," she's honking at the firefighter descending from the truck. Going crazy, bereft of manners or couth or much hearing, she sounds like a pissed-off goose most of the time. I've run into her occasionally in the leasing office, dropping off my rent check. "Hello," I'll say, and she'll just scowl as if I'm just taking another liter of her air away. "Oh, she's always like that," the office manager offers offhandedly. "Just the way she is."

The firefighter doesn't answer, but glances up at the furwad in the tree, makes a mental calculation of height, and takes an extension ladder off the truck. He leans it on the safest branch closest to the trunk, tests it with his weight, then begins climbing. The cat, by now, has ceased being nervous and is now curious. She looks down cautiously at the approaching stranger. When the firefighter is about four feet away, the cat does the unthinkable: It simply climbs down the tree. Quickly, too. A few halfhearted cheers from below, a few mumbled curses from the firefighter, and that's it. Except that by now, I'm just about perfectly in front of my window and the only person who notices is of course, AnnieFanny-GooseLady. Deaf as a post, but she can see everything. "And you put some clothes on, ya goddamn weirdo!" I feel my face get hot, then duck and cover. After I've convinced myself nobody else has seen me, I peek again at the parking lot. Most of the crowd is gone, and it's just the woman sitting on the curb with Molly.

She's cooing to the cat, rocking slowly back and forth. Even GooseLady is ambling back to her apartment. I finally do take my shower and check the window again. The two are still on the curb, even as the streetlights relieve the sun.

A week later, after a particularly ugly I-5 commute in the rain, I pull into my complex and see the fire truck again, with nearly the same crowd that showed up for the Great Cat Rescue. "Lovely. Which tree did that fat thing scale this week," I mumble, but the throng is more subdued, and there are police this time. I roll through slowly with my window down, trying to piece things together as much as trying to save the suspension of my car. Fragments, visual and spoken, fill in many gaps. I see two cops on either side of GooseLady, who's sitting on the curb, sobbing uncontrollably, choking out: ". . . cat was all she had . . ." I hear, ". . . poor girl. She wasn't right in the head to begin with . . ." ". . . I guess it really sent her over the edge . . ." " . . . goddamn pitbulls . . ." By the time I'm out of my car and on the first landing, my appetite is gone and my stomach is tight. By the time I'm in my apartment I've completed the puzzle. I go to the bedroom window, coat still zipped, shoes still on, and look out. The tree. The curb. I stand and I stare and I notice the streetlights have come on.

Gina

Bellevue is across the lake from Seattle, and very sensitive about being called a suburb. The wealth in Bellevue and neighboring Redmond is staggering, in a way it isn't in Seattle. The Eastside has its own culture, makes its own rules and its own billionaires. All the high-tech companies that matter are either headquartered along this little stretch of I-405, or they have major branches here. It lost a little of its luster at the dawn of the new millennium and the end of the honeymoon for upstart Internet companies, but per capita, the wealth is concentrated here. Bellevue. Kirkland. Medina. Hunts Point. Redmond. Issaquah. Moguls, sports stars, actors live and play here. Real estate is outrageously expensive, personalities are outrageously perky and polite, and people go out of their way to show you how rich they aren't. It is an enclave of the gloriously disconnected. And this is where Virginia Spencer lived.

Bellevue Square (BellSquare, in chic local parlance) wasn't your typical mall. In jaunty Bellevue style, it had the most exclusive stores (Barney's, FAO Shwartz, et al.), the most absurdly expensive jewelry, and the snottiest personnel. All done in an incredibly perky, "Oh, we're just like you little people," attitude that dripped from every storefront.

Gina wasn't your typical mall rat, though she hung out at Bell-Square quite a bit. School had let out three days earlier and she wanted to get down there as soon as Metro would take her from her mom's Eastside Prison of Neat. Gina wasn't typical because most 16 year old Mensa members don't hang out at BellSquare, hoping to get laid, methodically checking out all of the newest trends in retail technology. She was a tough sell to any hot blooded American male (or female, for that matter) teen, what with the ambivalent hygiene and eclectic piercings. She was hideous, somewhere between an emaciated Liza Minelli and a wet Manx cat. She really couldn't even play the "personality" card, because she instinctively repelled people. Nice wasn't in her nature. She had perfected the look that turns other humans into dried turds. It was as natural as eating an apple to her.

Her purpose in life for this particular summer day was to get to the mall and shock the Bellevue snobs by getting something else on her body pierced. She didn't know what; she'd figure that out when she got there.

As she shuffled her way to the Piercing Pod, she mentally inventoried which part of her she wanted pierced. Nipple? A possibility. That would have decent shock value. Yet it lent itself to being yanked too easily. Navel? Kinda trendy right now. Clitoris? Hmmm. That was about all that was left.

She remembered now that her bank's ATM was across the street. "Fuck," she said to the grotesque palm tree in the grotesque stone planter in front of her. "Too hot. I guess I'll eat the fee. What the fuck." She searched for the ATM closest to her electronics store of choice. "Shit. There used to be one right there." She stalked two storefronts past her Mecca and found a new, bigger ATM with a sharp blue stripe down the side. She sighed. The thought of paying an extra two bucks for the privilege of using somebody else's ATM was larceny, of course, but it was hot out there, cool in here, and the Pod kiosk was about thirty feet away. She could have used her debit card there, but she couldn't stand the thought of the store having that information about her—buying habits, all the psychographic stuff they use to target "personal" mass mailings.

She fished her cash card out of her lunchbox and stuck it in the appropriate slot. A warning flashed on the screen about how she was about to be charged a two dollar fee, blah, blah, blah—she hit the "OK" button. Another disclaimer came up. "In accordance. . ." blah, blah, blah—she hit the OK button again. "Fucking lawyers got everybody in the goddamn country scared of getting sued." Finally, the cash selection window came up. She entered the amount she wanted and stood at the machine like a teenager of the 1950s, playing pinball, hands resting on the edges, fingers over the flippers. She heard a beep and instinctively looked at the screen. She was greeted with a quick, sharp blast of light and a jolt to her palm. Suddenly, the machine was holding her cash out for her to take. She blinked a few times and took it. Something wasn't right. This was not cool. No. Something just happened.

She backed away from the machine without lifting her feet. She looked at her hands: Her right hand was actually bleeding. Not much, nearly imperceptible, but it was definitely blood. She could not explain why, but she felt violated. She felt the way she did when she got home from school one day and discovered somebody had broken into the house and stolen her mother's silver and jewelry. The eerie lingering ghost of thievery. All of this spun slowly on the Lazy Susan of fear inside her head.

She sat down on a bench in the middle of the causeway, staring in the direction of the ATM. "Fuck. Maybe it was just static." She shook her head and went back to get pierced.

Weeks passed, and the events at the mall gradually began to fade to the back of her consciousness like the music she listened to at work. She had begun to loosely rewrite her history of the event, much as TV journalists do if a story doesn't have enough flash. And Gina was becoming a TV audience for her own self-doubt.

After work one afternoon, she picked up her check from Mary The Accounting Geek at the back of the store and walked across the strip mall to her bank. She cashed her check there since her store was too small to support direct deposit, accurate bookkeeping, paid holidays, or actual benefits for people of part-time ilk. But she stuck around, sucked up the employee discounts, and socked away the rest in her Getaway Stash, which now approached the $8,000 dollar mark, with the addition of this particular check. "Oh, great," she sighed to herself as she entered the bank's lobby. "A whole stable of new teller cattle. Worse than McDonalds. Better pick a smart-looking, geeky one and hope it's not too painful." She quickly surveyed the staff behind the high counters for the human with the right criteria and found one with no customers. She grabbed a deposit slip and headed for this teller's window.

Once there, she nodded to the teller and took the pen that dangled from the little coiled cord to the right of the window and the teller's nameplate. Brian. She began filling out the deposit slip when she heard, "Oh, that's not necessary, Gina. You deposit regularly here. One-fifty-two fifty again?" Gina blinked. She looked at the deposit slip; she had only filled in the date and a few numbers. She hadn't signed it yet, nor had she entered her account number.

As she pondered that in a deepening daze, she heard herself say, "Um, yeah, but I wanted 20 bucks back in cash." And she resumed filling out the deposit slip, spinning her mental Rolodex, trying to figure out where Brian the Teller Geek could possibly have met her. But Brian persisted.

"No problem," he said, all bright and chipper. He plopped down a crisp new twenty-dollar bill and a transaction receipt right next to the incomplete deposit slip.

Gina gathered her wits a bit and said, "But how do you know—"

"We upgraded our system last week. Saves a ton of time, gets customers in and out in a flash. Have a great day. Enjoy the sun! We haven't had much lately."

Gina stumbled out of the bank and sat on a curb in the parking lot. Brian was right—the sun hadn't been out for nearly a week and it felt good on her face, pale though it was. She was still holding the twenty and the receipt in her hand. Suddenly, the ATM transaction made an ugly redux in her mind.

Home, she showered and avoided her parents. This wasn't particularly hard to do—her mother worked for one of the few DotComs that avoided euthanasia in the late '90s, and her father worked for an airline; she wasn't sure which one. The three of them were seldom in the house at the same time; indeed, the house was much like a beautiful, well-maintained suburban truck stop. The image oozed Bellevue perfection.

When one of them was home, Gina played the sullen, "you-wouldn't-understand-me-even-if-I-did-stoop-to talk-to-you" teen to a tee, and gave monosyllabic responses whenever the opportunity arose. Today, it was mom's turn.

"How was school today, Gina? You never mention it."

"Fine," she breathed. She was an honor student for the eleventh straight quarter.

"And work is okay? Getting along with everybody?"

"Yup." She was remarkably personable with perfect strangers.

"Getting enough sun? You look awfully pale, sweetie."

"Yes, mother." An exasperated sigh, followed by the patented teenage eye-roll.

"Well, I don't know—I mean, I never see you anymore . . . Look, I gotta get back to the office. We got a JAD session tonight. Buzz my cell if you need anything, okay?"

"Okay."

Gina's mom was in her early forties, very attractive, fit and toned with deep auburn hair and doe-like eyes, with mild but defined curves, and utterly bereft of sensuality. It was this kind of calculated presence that Gina loathed, even as much as she loved her mother. She wasn't mature enough to articulate it, let alone in a positive way, so the disapproval manifested itself in piercings, isolation, and the burgeoning desire to hump any mammal that crossed her path.

She glanced out the window in time to see the Lexus SUV back out of the driveway and coast to the stop sign at the end of the street, then blend into the idyllic afternoon. She lazily back-flopped onto the overstuffed leather sofa and stared up at the vaulted ceiling and its exposed beams. She found the remote control for the stereo burrowing into her back, so she arched and pulled it out, pressing the "Power" button at the same time. She didn't have a good grip on it, and the remote clattered to the shiny maple floor. She thought about getting it, but in the end, she just wanted noise anyway, so she waited for whatever sound was about to come blaring out of the surround-sound speakers. It was the news on NPR. Again, she wanted to get up and change stations, but the sofa had a pretty good grip by now, and she wanted to be held. She sank into the leather, closed her eyes and began to detach. Until . . . about a third of the way into a particular monologue . . . her eyes opened.

". . . Industries is declaring a moral and financial victory today just two months after its IPO. The ATM manufacturer, in cooperation with local and federal anti-terrorist groups, has pioneered what it terms as 'the world's first pluralistic secured-ID automated teller machines, or 'pee-sid ay tee ems,' for short. Customers are read a standard disclaimer about how the information gathered from them will be used to prevent terrorism at home and abroad. Customers are not told, however, exactly who will have access to this information, and that the sale of such information is perfectly legal under the New Freedom Act, passed shortly after 9/11. Civil liberties groups and liberal organizations nationwide have decried the idea since its inception . . ."

Gina's mind shut down again. She felt cold. Queasy. SecuriNex was a new company; she couldn't help but hear about it. It had made a big splash in the community about a year earlier, buying up abandoned Boeing buildings in the Bellevue area, hiring absurd masses of people in the teeth of an economic recession, tossing PSAs all over radio and TV, focusing on how easy and convenient security can be. The ads were so vague and homey, most people didn't bother trying to figure out what product was being sold, and wrote it off as another high-tech company doing a flaky ad for the geek population, which is substantial in GatesLand. There were bus posters, banners, signs, billboards, and all had little more than obscure messages about security, families, and brilliant ideas. And the slick, Eurostyle tagline, "Be the wave."

Soon it was dark and after awhile she drifted in and out of sleep on the huge sofa, alternating nightmares and erotic dreams. In between, she decided to learn more about this company, SecuriNex. That would have to wait until morning. She wasn't working, it was mid-July, and she was a teenager. Sometimes, it had its advantages.

Days off for Gina usually meant sleeping until noon, a quick, muffled session with her vibrator, and an excursion via mass transit. Today was slightly different; she didn't sleep until noon, but just long enough to hear her mother leave for work. She showered quickly, grabbed her lunchbox and headed to the bus stop. She stood next to the Eastside's elite: Neatly clipped corporate casual male and female, Eddie Bauer and Land's End, both vaguely aware that riding a bus is better than driving alone, but acutely aware that it was a popular trend to treat the planet well as they pursued obscene amounts of personal wealth while being obeisant whores to a large corporation. Gina wrote them off as harmless DINKs and commenced ignoring them almost immediately. Their bus arrived, heading downtown. Gina instinctively reached inside her lunchbox for her bus pass, and was pissed off that it wasn't there. It took so much time to find the correct change for these damn fareboxes. The bus door opened and the DINKs climbed aboard. Gina ascended the steps slowly behind them, as she tried to come up with the correct change. She braced herself gently by holding the polished handrail that led up the steps. The bus driver, barely giving her a second glance, said, "This only goes downtown. No upgrades." Before she could say, "Huh?" the bus driver, again, barely acknowledging her presence, said, "Regional passes are good for peak travel in this zone. You're fine. Have a nice day."

Gina staggered to her seat and plopped in it, like a hastily dropped bag of groceries. Her mind reeled. As she was trying to make sense of this latest mindfuck, a similarly-pierced young buck leaned over the seat and said, "Cool, ain't it?"

Gina just glared at him.

"I mean, shit, you don't have to remember anything. Keys, cards, passes—it's cool shit, no?"

"What the fuck are you talking about?"

"Well, you been pinned, right?"

"What?"

"Pinned. You got the chip, the code."

"Are you high?"

"Well, you wouldna got on this bus without it."

"Without what?" Gina's denial gradually turned to panic, and her mouth went dry.

"Wow. You don't know, do ya? Some people don't. Yeah, you got this chip in the palm a your hand. It's about half the size of a grain of Uncle Ben's. Any place that participates-they know you."

Gina just stared.

"So anyway, that's why you don't need no pass anymore."

"How do you know this shit?"

"Dad. Works at the 'Nex. He's a PR dude."

Gina decided to take a detour to the mall.

It was one of those brilliantly sunny days with big white cotton candy clouds scattered here and there. She got off the bus amid condescending stares and muffled chatter. "Probably too hopped up to know about what's really going on in the country."

"Yeah. Probably lives on the street or something."

She heard some comments, ignored others, didn't care about any of them. The mall wasn't open yet, so she sat on a bench outside, opened up her lunchbox and pulled out a pen and started scribbling notes. "Work," then "Nex." She tilted her face toward the sun for a moment, and closed her eyes. When she opened them, they fixated lazily on a small plane high above SeaTac's flight paths. There was something strange about it she couldn't quite place. Its shape was somewhat normal, except for the squared wing tips. It was silent, but that was due, most likely, to its incredible altitude. Maybe it was the speed; the damn thing seemed to be just hanging there. Another plane flew well below it, much closer to the horizon, at a much more normal speed, looking like a normal plane. Probably a fighter from McChord. It ascended sharply, leveled off, and ejected an object that looked to be roughly the size and shape of a VW Beetle. It looked like it should have dropped, but it stayed up there, floating among the scattered clouds. The fighter peeled away in a dramatic arc and descended to a relative position several thousand feet below and behind the little Bug. On the ground, other people began to notice this activity, too, and while some stopped and stared, most just muttered smugly about the new detection systems and went about their business. Gina heard the comments but none of it really registered; she was still trying to make sense of the impromptu airshow going on 50,000 feet above her head. A few Corporate Casuals sipping chai tea in Starbucks cups nodded sagely and remarked on the satellite sentry and how it could even operate despite gravity and drag. Then, as if scripted, the square-winged jet streaked silently across the fluffy clouds as the satellite made its quiet arc southward, hundreds of miles away from the plane. Suddenly the satellite held position and spat something toward a bank of cumulus far in advance of the plane's path. As the little jet disappeared into the clouds, those on the ground noticed lightning-like flashes for a few seconds, but otherwise the clouds held steady, the blue background held steady, and all was normal again in the summer sky again. The satellite gradually drifted above the atmosphere into oblivion. Out of sight, out of mind, as was the fighter. Gina wondered about the plane, though. She didn't see it conclusively explode, but she never saw it pass completely through the cloud, either. It just wasn't there anymore. No wreckage, no sounds, no great fireball. Or was this all new, too?

What she saw in the sky didn't shock her. What she saw on the ground did. *The people*. This was little more than the Blue Angels doing their pre-SeaFair warmups over Lake Washington, the way they do every year. *The people*. This was watching BP at Safeco Field. They sipped their lattes, walked their dogs, talked on cell phones, drove badly, bitched about their jobs. The comments she could actually hear amounted to, "It's about time they do something like that."

She noticed that the mall had been open for about a half-hour when she finally looked toward the main entrance. Even there, something earth-shattering hadn't taken place. An incredibly sophisticated and highly destructive defense system hadn't just been displayed for hundreds of thousands of common people to witness, should they but look up. Just Tuesday morning, mid-July, Bellevue Washington. Bill Gates' back yard. The mall. She went in and sprinted down the length of the mall to find the ATM she used that afternoon three weeks ago. It wasn't there. But there were six of them by the Food Court. Out of breath, she approached it cautiously. Without touching the machine, she jutted her chin toward the little screen to read what was on it. Some ads. Secure a new home loan through Bank of America. Buy a CD with fantastic returns. Personal lines of credit. Then it started over. With nothing further at stake, she pulled her ATM card out of her lunchbox and swiped it through the slot. The fee disclaimer came up. She very carefully pressed the appropriate button to acknowledge it with her house key. Then she saw the second disclaimer:

"In accordance with the New Freedom Act, all persons making cash withdrawals from this automated teller machine may be subject to anti-terrorism security measures including retinal recording, genetic indexing, audio sampling and other safeguards as technology allows. Your freedom and safety are important to us, so please indicate your acceptance of these terms by tapping the screen as indicated below or pressing the blue button to the left of this panel. Thank you for using SecuriNex Personal Tellers."

Gina went cold. She stared at the machine, unblinking, for interminable seconds. She started to shake and stammer. "No," she finally managed. "No. No. You can't do this." She normally wasn't given to self-consciousness, but she looked around. One middle-aged woman looked at her oddly and finally said, "Honey, they're doing this everywhere. It's perfectly safe and legal. If it keeps 'em out, isn't it worth it?"

Ed And The Evil Garden Gnome

Ed was just numb.

He had been mowing his lawn - an arduous three-hour job complicated by all the oddly-placed debris and ornaments his wife had collected at garage sales - and was carefully trying to avoid murdering one of those damn lawn gnomes behind the old cedar. He didn't hear the explosion above the noise of the fiercely laboring mower, and he didn't see it due to his intense but begrudging attention to gnome preservation. Had he turned around, he would have experienced a visual treat: An entire 30-gallon water heater shooting through his garage roof, arcing gracefully above a power line or two, clearing the Ebersole's driveway, and gouging a splendid crater where the Stevenson's dahlias used to be. But no, he had been concentrating on the big gnome with the dumb sleepy grin, in a posture that suggested he was supposed to be leaning against the base of a tree or something, preparing for a nap.

Not this one, this one was free-standing about two feet from the tree. No sooner did he swiftly nudge it out of harm's way with his left foot than the mower came to an abrupt and clanking halt. Startled and swearing, Ed had pulled the mower away from the accident site. "Damn damn damn piece of godd--" Apparently, he had neglected the large plastic Ladybug-on-a-Stick that never did stand up straight. Now, muttering at the shards of red plastic in the grass and wire wrapped around the spindle of his lawnmower, he had finally said, "Screw it," and headed to the house for a beverage or two.

The backyard is pretty private, so he hadn't noticed people dashing this way and that along his street in front of his house: gaping at the now-tattered garage and exit wound in the roof, and trotting over to the Stevenson's place to see the new Andy Warhol gardening exhibit. He paused in the rear entry to take off his grass-stained sneakers and ignore the little voice telling him something was amiss. Didn't take him long to figure it out, though: The cat, Ellie, a normally sedate tabby who found it perfectly exhausting to stand while she ate, was hunched in a ball behind the woodstove, not moving, eyes wide and still. "What the . . ." his voice trailed off as he headed toward the living room, adjacent to the garage. A few things were out of place in the kitchen; things off shelves, doors open. Still not enough to get his full attention. And then: The living room. Glass everywhere. TV smashed, plaster cracked and falling, furniture jostled, and to his dismay, he could now see his workbench, which would not be possible had the door to the garage from the living room still been on its hinges.

Stupefied, he stumbled back to the family room to gather up the cat and try to soothe them both. Now, standing in the threshold of the living room entry to the garage, he merely stared at the scene. As he did this, a good-sized chunk of ceiling had just about freed itself from its moorings above his head and then, WHUMP. Fortunately, it hit him squarely enough that it broke apart on impact, and while it did drive him to his knees, it didn't knock him out. Ellie was less impressed. On impact, she saw fit to swipe Ed's neck, narrowly missing the carotid. Still, there was a fair amount of blood, and the wound, now mixed with plaster and sweat, began to sting and throb. He picked up Ellie again after a tense moment and headed out through the garage.

Nothing was in one piece. Everything had become shrapnel embedded in sheetrock. Wood, plaster, laundry, tools - all were layered on the floor in varying states of dismemberment. Still awestruck, he managed to feel warmth on the top of his head. His bald spot was telling him this was sun, but that was impossible, of course, because he was in his gar- He looked up and gawked at the bright blue summer sky offering its calming presence. After a bit of that he made his way toward the big garage door that had all its panels blown out. Tiptoeing carefully on his bare feet, he noticed a curious little boy of about four pawing his way through the rubble just outside the garage. Behind him by about thirty feet was a paramedic trotting up to the scene. "Sir, you need to get out of there right away." It was the mere sight of the paramedic that snapped him to attention and made him move too quickly. He tripped over a plastic flamingo and lurched forward, sending Ellie flying for freedom. Since he knew wherever he landed inside the garage would hurt plenty, he made a bit of a lunge at the last second to avoid such a fate. In doing so, he leveled the little boy in front of him, causing him to scream. Then Ed screamed, too. Not for the scraped elbows he endured when he landed on the petaled concrete of his driveway, but for the machete that sliced his calf open after falling from its precarious perch above the big garage door. Through the searing pain he heard cries of "Did you see that!?" "Woulda speared him in the head!" "Saved the kid AND the damn cat!" "It was God himself in there. God did that!"

Moments later, on the stretcher, Ed was numb. He was still numb as the first microphones were shoved under his nose and still more numb as the powerful lights blasted his line of sight. "Sir! How does it feel to be a hero? Are you going to sue the water heater company? Do you feel any hostility toward the manufacturer? Have you always had an abiding love for cats? Sir, can you describe what's going through your mind right now?"

There was a tense silence as the reporters finally stopped shouting questions at Ed and waited for a ripe soundbite. Ed stammered a bit and blinked into the lights. "I . . . I . . . uh. . . . I uh, . . . uh . . . I just wanted a beer."

My Father's Sword

In a crappy little house in southeastern New Hampshire, tucked
away in the crude joists and cobbled wiring, you'll find a sheathed
bayonet from the Korean War. From a real, dead Korean soldier.
I know. I put it there. No, I'm not the veteran. That would be my
father.

I had a pretty nifty little model railroad in my parent's basement
when I was a kid. Rolling hills, rocky cuts and even a little switch-
ing yard. I still have a substantial trivial knowledge of railroading
and history. One day, though, when I was about 12, I had gotten
a little too tricky for my own good with wiring the remote con-
trolled switches in the yard. I was stumped. Then, as I still do
today when things get difficult, I took a deep breath and tilted my
head back and looked up at the "ceiling." That's in quotes because
the main floor of the house was thrown together by a bachelor in
the early '30s, then added onto when my parents bought it in the
'60s. It was a patchwork of rough-hewn timbers and utility-pole
trimmings, as well as a few actual joist-sized pieces in there. This
was braced with whatever other scraps were left over, which created all sorts of cubbies and crannies for spiders to multiply. But
on this occasion, when I looked up, I looked in a slightly different
place and something caught my eye. I could probably reach it
unaided today, but then I dragged a sawhorse under the spot
I wanted to reach and hopped up on it. I pulled on the thing; it
was . . . wooden? Well, sort of . . . then I saw the handle. Wow!
A sword in a scabbard. Without even thinking about it, I dropped
down, and started running up the stairs, thinking about what
something like this was worth and if this was archeology, it was
pretty cool, and I wonder what other museum stuff I could find,
and I burst into the kitchen, wanting to show this to anybody in
the house.

As it happened, my father was standing there, just about to pour
a cup of coffee. I was out of breath, partly from running up the
stairs, but mostly from the sheer excitement of this little piece of
history in my hands. I just blurted out, "Look at this!" He turned
around. His facial expression didn't change much, but it felt like
somebody opened the door to the freezer. He was way too quiet,

so I said, "Do you know what it is?" His half-mumbled reply hit me like a small bag of flour. "Yeah, I got that off a guy . . ." I stood there for a few extra seconds expecting ". . . in the War," ". . . for twenty bucks in Korea," ". . . in combat," but those turned out to be the only words he ever said about that War that carried any meaning. He had talked about being in the Service, about being overseas, about being on boats during his Tour, but this . . . I was chilled by it. It wasn't the jovial bitching about cramped quarters and stupid soldiers and being a tough Marine. This was right from the psyche. I had no idea what I'd done, but I knew it wasn't good. I couldn't possibly have gauged what was in his mind then, not through the eyes of a 12-year-old kid in a crappy little town in a crappy little house in southeastern New Hampshire.

I turned around and was about to ask him about it some more, but he had disappeared into the living room and his chair and the local paper, which always meant, "Further examination or discussion is strongly discouraged." He read the paper a lot. Not to say he was a grump or didn't like anybody. But he reveled in his comforts. The paper. The chair. The cellar. Sports. And unfortunately, booze.

And just like that, he was done. I don't think my mother ever knew about it.

I stood there at the threshold of the living room and looked at the meaningless headlines on the crappy little town's newspaper. Yup, he's reading, all right. Thoroughly deflated and bewildered, I decided there was really nothing left to do but go back downstairs and put the damn thing back where I found it. Which I did.

I didn't want to work on my railroad anymore; I sat on the sawhorse and stared up at the hilt of that thing in the makeshift joists. I did my best, with the maturity and experience of a 12-year-old, to analyze what had just happened from a psychological and emotional point of view. I was kind of sad. A little worried. I had never seen him respond like that to anything. I simultaneously didn't know what I had done, and I knew exactly what I had done. I just couldn't articulate it. How did he get it, and why wouldn't he talk about it? I thought it was kinda cool that I had found it; now I felt like I had barged in while he was going to the bathroom or something. Twelve years old, trying to be introspective, failing. Trying to picture combat. Failing. Intensely curious about an object that old, and wanting desperately to ask questions of the one person who had just clearly demonstrated he would *never* talk about it. So I ended up doing what I always did when he hid behind that paper. I "forgot" about it and pretended everything had just returned to normal.

I can't remember if that particular incident changed anything for him. He still drank in the basement, drowning whatever emotions happened to crop up. He still hid behind that crappy newspaper in full view of my mother and me. He'd yell or cheer at football players (pro and college) ,second-guess Red Sox pitchers, or talk back to the TV newscast. Typical stuff. For him. For us.

There he was, the Marine, doing the Manual of Arms with my BB gun under the clothesline. There he was, bitching loudly about Jimmy Carter and his spinelessness. There he was, in a chair in the police station with his second DUI, now without a license. There he was, at my sister's wedding reception, trying to do one-armed push-ups alongside somebody half his age. There he was, telling me I couldn't borrow the car because he'd just been too permissive with me lately. There he was, never giving in, never showing up, never allowing a soul in. Or out.

He escaped in football, basketball, baseball, booze, and hockey. He devoured every newspaper put in front of him, even if the journalism sucked. He loved dogs and me and I suppose my mother. He was fluent in French, English, and Denial.

He worked whatever jobs he could find, after his stint in the Korean War, to keep us afloat in the sixties and early seventies. I remember him in construction, at the brick factory, in the kitchen at the VA hospital, and finally, as a foreman of a spill crew on nuclear powered submarines. He hated every last one of his jobs. Wouldn't say it, didn't have to; it was etched in everything he did. Cynicism about his bosses, equal opportunity employment, and bureaucracy. Suspicion about neighbors. The fellow Catholic churchgoers he'd call phonies under his breath in the parking lot after Mass. The out-loud speculation that the phony priest was a pedophile. The only solace he really found was in the rotgut whiskey he'd hide all over the house, the crappy little newspaper of my hometown, and the cheap reclining chair in his corner of the living room.

He demanded perfection but didn't expect it. I was a decent athlete in high school, but I never got to hear him tell me that. "What happened?" is what I'd hear if I lost a tight tiebreaker in tennis, went 2-for-3 in baseball, missed the net once in soccer. "You think she's cute," was the retort I'd hear after shyly bringing a date home while in high school. "You'll never finish college," and "You can't make any money writing" were the snide mantras of my adolescence. It was my job to understand these as prods of encouragement; if I succeeded at both, he'd say I understood him. If I failed, he'd be right - not disappointed.

He drank and drove, drove and drank. Hid vodka under the front seat right next to his emotions. Carried on dialogues with sports-talk radio hosts while sitting in the car, in our driveway, in the dark, after another screamfest with my mother. I'd creep out there after a while to see if everything was OK and to make sure none of what was happening was my fault. He'd throw his arm around me or tousle my hair to let me know I'd be all right, but I never knew if he was.

When he was sober, he was smart and curious. He read historical novels and was a big Michener fan. His political opinions were well founded, since he devoured news from any medium at any time. When he was sober, he had a sense of humor that was wry and crisp and genuinely zany. He was generous with physical affection as a way of compensating for the lack of kind words. When he was sober, this was perfectly fine with me.

He loved us. He was the one trying like an idiot, me alongside, to bodysurf ski-boat wakes in Lake Winnipesaukee. He was the one, flipping me over his shoulder in the warm water, and standing there to make sure I came up laughing. He was the one who shared my fascination with video games when they first came out. He was the one I overheard telling one of his friends what a genius I was.

He chain-smoked Pall Malls, couldn't care less about a healthy diet, and drank himself to death before he turned sixty.

Ten years ago.

But timing in real life never makes as much sense as in movies, and revelations often get away before they're properly grasped. That sword. That damned sword.

He was already an alcoholic by the time I was twelve, but the day I found the sword he was perfectly sober. Lucky for me; not knowing what kind of reception I'd have gotten otherwise. No, while I was trying to make sense of all the information presented me in the previous ten minutes or so, he was in the living room, reading the paper. Truthfully, I couldn't see his face, just the four fingers on either hand at three and nine o'clock—the Classic Position, as I had come to call it as a teenager—but I had no reason to believe that's not exactly what he was doing. He was just built like that. Or was he?

By twelve I had suspected there was a problem with his drinking; by thirteen, I knew. And even then, I had always wondered: What put him on that path to begin with? My mother? Well, she wasn't the easiest person to get along with in a crappy little house in a crappy little town. That was true enough. But she couldn't have been the sole reason he numbed himself with alcohol. Low pay, menial, dead-end jobs? Yeah, that may have been a catalyst, perhaps. But things like that are usually the toppings on a really bad dessert, not the rotten entree. No, these weren't IT, and in retrospect, I think I began to understand that day, that there was a large part of my father's life I would never understand, never know, never reach. And he wanted it that way.

During snow days from school, I'd go down there to work on my railroad, invariably screw something up or get bored, and end up looking at the hilt of that sword, sticking out of that cubby. I had managed to put some distance between The Encounter and my curiosity, and my imagination began to take over. I imagined he had killed a Korean soldier to get it, of course. Then it became him crawling through a battlefield and grabbing it off a dead Korean just in time to defend himself from a live one; then another variation, and another and another until I got pissed off with my own delusions and thought, "Why didn't he just tell me about it?"

Years went by and adolescence took over. The railroad gradually went away as high school sports occupied my spare time. I'd still wander through that part of the cellar on my way to get to the lawn mower or other garden implement, and I'd always check to see if it was still there. Yup. At one point he must have gone on a painting binge because a good portion of the "ceiling" had been painted white, and the sword had been removed and replaced hilt-first, and one side of the scabbard now had cheap white semi-gloss paint on it. But it was still there in its home. Still nagging me. Still whispering, "I'll never tell. Never."

But my father became a project for me after that. His alcoholism became more pronounced, and my parents' marriage deteriorated in geometric progression. Being in the house for any length of time became a chore, a burden and a sentence. I vowed two things: I would get out of that house, that town, that state, as soon as I could afford to. I would figure out why he was the way he was. Little did I know that the former would be a day at the beach compared to the latter.

Years later, on my own, I crashed. I couldn't concentrate. I meandered. I stood in the driveway with my parents one rainy summer morning in the driveway of that little yard after years of vowing to myself I'd get out of that crappy little house. As always, the exit never had the same emotion. I had wanted it to be a glorious thing, cathartic and righteous, with a sense of permanence and closure. As it happened, I was only able to take away symbols of those.

We stood in the driveway, my parents and I, as my friend Allan sat in the front seat of the little U-Haul truck. My mother was crying and incoherent. I'm amazed now as I was then that my father was, too. He actually did pull it together long enough to choke out the words, "I love you. I'm proud of you." It would be the last time I heard those words, and I knew even then how hard it was to say them. I remember crying a little, but those tears were quickly swallowed by the pure exhilaration of the adventure I had just begun.

But I arrived at my destination with no idea how to proceed. It was a matter of, "Now what?" I had no tools to deal with the questions my father had raised, both through the terseness of his interactions with me regarding that war or anything else, for that matter. At one point, I focused on the alcoholism, because that was the thing, I had decided, that had stolen so much of my childhood and was the center of so much of my rage and fear. A year or so of confronting codependence in terms of my relationships with women and in terms of my relationship with him brought me some comfort and understanding, but most questions persisted. What was he thinking? Why wasn't I good enough? What pleased him? Why did he start drinking in the first place? Am I predisposed to be like him? For my own sanity, I enlisted the help of ACA and lots of self-help reading. All brought comfort and a semblance of structure to my life, but the feeling was short-lived, at most. It provided the proper survival tools to push the real answers farther out of my reach, and at the time, that was perfectly fine with me.

During that time, my mind would wander back to that sword and that house and those times with a furtiveness I was never comfortable with. There were the times he'd disappear downstairs ostensibly to start some project or other, but my mother and I knew what he had hidden down there. He'd come up either minutes or hours later, either slightly or extremely altered, dashing any hopes I had that he might actually be working on something down there. Nope, just his private reserve. It started as whiskey and then became vodka. I couldn't then, and I still can't fathom the depth of pain he was trying to drown or burn.

There were the times he'd "go to the store" and come back slightly or extremely altered, and my mother and I knew where his trip had taken him. It was no secret, yet he insisted on the pretense. I always felt slighted when he didn't take me, and my mother had long since stopped asking, but we both knew the facts. We just didn't know the reasons.

There were also the good times, which I'd like to keep as him sober, and my mom and I happy participants. Sometimes this was the case, but I know I could tinker with those memories enough to take the murkiness of recall away. I choose not to. I see us all at Lake Winnipesaukee, trying like idiots to bodysurf the wakes of ski boats while my mother grilled burgers up on the uneven shore. He'd fling me around in the warm water and the oppressive New England humidity, and everything would disappear into silliness and summer. These moments are still lifes for me, and I take them everywhere and display them proudly when I smile or wrestle with my own son on my living room floor. I don't have many, but the ones I do own are crisp with detail and emotion. I can only hope he had the same ones and felt them the way I do.

I will never pretend to understand what my father or others like him went through. What that sword represented, like it or not, was horror. It was something concrete he could keep in a safe place, next to the spiders and loose bottles of whiskey. No value in releasing that sort of toxicity on innocent civilians. I bet it's similar to today's inner city police officers, but how can I know? I've never witnessed soul-robbing violence first hand, never been in a fight, let alone a war.

I'm going back to that little hick town in southeastern New Hampshire next fall. Visit my mom, see the fall colors. My mother remarried a few years ago and lives with the complete opposite of my father in a little apartment not too far from the little house where I grew up. I wonder if I'll have the courage to peek in on the new owners of that house, and perhaps ask politely for a look in the basement. See if I can reach that sword one more time, wherever it is.

Afterword

According to the Korean Studies Center at UCAL-Berkeley, there were well over two million civilian casualties, mostly North Korean. About 500,000 North Korean and 55,000 American soldiers were killed, along with about a million Chinese. For me, it remains a bitter irony that there was no clear or moral victory in this war, that the area is still hotly disputed, and that for all its apparent "necessity," The Korean War has a conspicuous absence in American historical conscience. But what it did to soldiers and families on both sides is irrefutable and permanent.

Writing About Life in Keith's Own Words

I do have a voice; some have called it unique and powerful. I do believe I have the talent for this sort of thing; it borders on cockiness sometimes. Write about life.

Mine? I've had it up to my ass with writing about me. Life in general? I guess. I like to observe, learn and report. I guess I'm pretty good at it. I notice things. I watch. I listen. Strange things intrigue me. I want to see behind the language, I want to see through the image and get to the foundations. I don't want to know God's thoughts, I want to know how God got to be god and what idiot put him in charge. I want to prove that there's always something new under the sun.

So I sit and write in public spaces. I scrawl poetry in cheap notebooks while I sit in my aging minivan. I whack out drivel on my AlphaSmart 300 while sitting in a Starbucks or worse. I write with zeal about nothing, about everything. I write, therefore, I am? Not quite that grandiose, perhaps. But it is a part of me more so than most folks.

My purpose as a writer, as poet: bring beauty to the world by showing the facets of life by carefully crafting words to frame visions and vistas that are always here, but need pointing to. It is, as some Zen teachings might suggest, the finger pointing at the moon.

So don't do the dog thing and stare at the finger.

About the Author

Keith Raymond Deshaies was born on November 17, 1964 in Rochester, New Hampshire to Raymond and Claire Deshaies. Keith grew up in Somersworth, New Hampshire where he developed a lifelong enthusiasm for trains, a gift for wood working and a love of the written word.

He relocated to the Seattle area in 1986, where he spent time in the Japanese studies department at the University of Puget Sound. Keith was an avid bicyclist, completing the Seattle to Portland race in 1989. From 1990—1999, Keith lived in the Bellingham area with is first wife, Laurel, and their two children, Becca and Aaron. In 2000, Keith completed the Excellence Series through the Excellence Foundation where he met his wife, Jennifer. In 2005, he returned to the Bellingham area and converted to Buddhism. He actively participated in local and national politics, most recently becoming a Senior Managing Editor for Northwest Progressive Institute. Keith was employed by Comcast for the last 10 years of his life as a Business and IT Analyst. Keith died of a massive heart attack on April 4, 2008 in his home. His love of quirky humor, vast intelligence, and fondness for fountain pens will be remembered and missed by all who love him.

At the end of a recent journal, he described himself:

I am a Democratic Socialist Buddhist Technical Writing Novelist wannabe with sleep apnea and migraines with a great family, great house, great life, really, and I don't want to stop until I've changed the world.